Coast to Coast

Dalesman Publishing Company
Stable Courtyard, Broughton Hall,
Skipton, North Yorkshire BD23 3AE

First Edition 1998

Text © Ronald Turnbull 1998
Cover: Fremington Edge, near Reeth, Swaledale,
by Deryck Hallam
Maps by Martin Collins
Printed by Midas Printing (HK) Ltd

A British Library Cataloguing in Publication
record is available for this book

ISBN 185568 1013 √

Coast to Coast

Ronald Turnbull

Series Editor Terry Marsh

DALESMAN

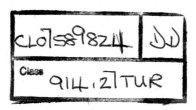

Publisher's Note
The information given in this book has been provided in
good faith and is intended only as a general guide. Whilst
all reasonable efforts have been made to ensure that details
were correct at the time of publication, the author and
Dalesman Publishing Company Ltd cannot accept any
responsibility for inaccuracies. It is the responsibility of individuals undertaking outdoor activities to approach the
activity with caution and, especially if inexperienced, to do
so under appropriate supervision. They should also carry
the appropriate equipment and maps, be properly clothed
and have adequate footwear. The sport described in this
book is strenuous and individuals should ensure that they
are suitably fit before embarking upon it.

Contents

Dedication

Guidebook writers don't matter – even Wainwright doesn't matter. Any long walk in England must link the uplands by rights of way through the valleys: the pink dotted lines on the map. The people who make this possible are the ones who field by field and stile by stile are making those pink dots into usable paths, adjusting them onto more sensible or more scenic lines, repairing what we trample and creating new ways where necessary. They work for public bodies, private landowners and charities. Along the Coast-to-Coast, they are:

Cumbria County Council; West Cumbria Groundwork Trust; SUSTRANS; the Countryside Commission; Forestry Commission (Grizedale, Pickering); Lake District National Park; the National Trust; Lancrigg Guest House; North West Water; East Cumbria Countryside Project; Lowther Estates; the gentleman from Crosby Garrett with the secateurs; Yorkshire Dales National Park; North Yorkshire County Council; Cleveland Way Project; North York Moors National Park; individual parish and borough councils; and others who work so discreetly as not to have come to my attention. These are:

THE PEOPLE WHO LOOK AFTER THE PATH.

Introduction

The Coast-to-Coast Walk was invented by Alfred Wainwright, amended and rendered largely legal by later walkers, and, lately, smoothed and improved by National Parks and Local Authorities. There's general agreement that it is the best long walk south of Scotland.

It has an inspiring idea: Irish Sea to the North one (or, perhaps even better, the other way round). It has an inspiring line: bang through the middle of three great upland areas. It's just the right length: serious but not impossible, a fortnight's holiday for the fit and a once-in-a-lifetime achievement for the rest of us. And when you get down to the detail, the country between St Bees and Bay Town is not just surprisingly beautiful, but beautiful in a surprising number of different ways.

A good walk is a story, and any good story has sad bits. The Coast-to-Coast will bring difficulty, and some suffering, and it would be a poorer walk if it didn't. You are, after all, walking right across a country. It's the red clifftops of St Bees and it's the romantic cragged hollows of Lakeland. It's the challenging slopes of Haweswater and the green ways across the limestone. It's the ravaged ravines and intricate stone walls of Swaledale, but also the golden masonry of Richmond; the small sharp peaks of Cleveland, the brown moors and sudden green valleys; and the clustered red roofs of Robin Hood's Bay. It takes you over two mountains and four high passes; through fourteen woods; past seven waterfalls; and over eight stone footbridges – some will like best the elegantly-arched Beggar's Bridge, others the balanced single slab at Gunnerside Gill. It's a walk where a moderate amount of effort is rewarded with a disproportionate amount of delight.

PLANNING THE WALK

It's roughly 190 miles (300km) from the Irish Sea to the North Sea. How you do them depends on your speed, and how much you want to carry: whether you break the journey or do it in one: whether you like tents, houses, or even green plastic bags. These matters are dealt with below.

One overall thought: the snail carries his home on his back. But the snail doesn't move very rapidly. We can't say how much the snail enjoys himself along the way, but the walker with less than 20lbs/10 kg up finds it much easier to have fun. (Packs of over 30lbs/15 kg are nothing but a struggle. I'd throw away even the most necessary of luxuries to stay below 30lbs.) So use the B&Bs, or the luggage transport services. This should be a treat, not a trudge.

Is backwards better? Realists travel eastwards. Wind, rain, even the occasional sleet and snow come from the west, and expend their fury on the realist's rucksack rather than on the realist himself (or herself). Idealists travel west: for while all the walk is good, Lakeland is best and it does make sense to save this till last. Also, if you reach Shap feeling fighting fit and frisky, you can finish in style by taking in a dozen high peaks on the way out to the Irish Sea. (On the other hand, if you reach Shap blistered and miserable, Lakeland will finish you off.) Ninety per cent of the walkers seem to be realists, which may be a sad reflection on the days we live in, or merely on the fact that people don't like reading their guidebooks upside-down.

For idealists I have added a description of the walk backwards: this is certainly the romantic direction, and the one I chose myself for my first crossing. I've assumed that you idealists are rather more experienced walkers, and given you a lighter style of guidebook: those comfort-loving realists would complain if I doubled the weight of their guidebook for the sake of a few perverse reversers.

ACCOMMODATION

Beer, bath and bed occur every ten to fifteen miles (15 to 20 km) – except in the Cleveland Hills, and there are ways of dealing with the Cleveland Hills.

Campsites are abundant; some well-equipped, others mere field corners. Wild camping is possible only in the Lake District National Park. Here it is tolerated, provided you do it at altitude and move on after a single night leaving no trace.

On the other hand, places with roofs on are also abundant, ranging from three-star hotels, through B&Bs and youth hostels to the humble camping barn at £3.25 per night. This accommodation is heavily used: Keld, where the Pennine Way crosses, has been booked solid as early as April.

You can book in advance, possibly through one of the booking bureaus I have listed. This ties you to a schedule, which is annoying if you get terrifically fit and want to start doing two days at a time. Alternatively, you can hope for the best. Outside the main English holiday season (July-August) you will usually manage to find a bed for tonight, this morning. However, you may have to wander off the route, and at worst you might be forced into a romantic night out under the stars or a dripping hedge-end.

About half the walkers who start start on a Saturday. This means that accommodation in Ennerdale Bridge is scarce on a Saturday night; at Borrowdale, on a Sunday – and that Shap is at its busiest on a Wednesday night. If you like your fellow-walker, start on a Saturday.

PUBLIC TRANSPORT

There is good transport to just four points on the walk. St Bees and Kirkby Stephen lie on two of England's most attractive railways; Grasmere is served by express coaches. Robin Hood's Bay is a short bus ride from Whitby and a third lovely railway. It is quicker (but less pretty) to leave Robin Hood's Bay by bus to Middlesbrough or Scarborough.

WALKING CONDITIONS AND WEATHER

Autumn and winter crossings are for specialists. They will require thigh-length gaiters (for mud), powerful torches (for getting benighted), winter equipment (for blizzards), a sense of humour and a high pain threshold. The route is busiest during the holiday months of July and August. These are fairly wet months, and when not wet, can be uncomfortably hot. The best weather is likely to be in April, May or June.

In April and early May there is a chance of snow on the high Lakeland passes, and even on Nine Standards Rigg. Snow and mist together make navigation very much more serious, and getting lost in snow on the Kidsty Pike crossing could land you on steep, exposed ground. To a lesser extent, it could on the Grasmere-Borrowdale pass as well. I have given an alternative route around the Kidsty Pike section.

Early in the year, new grass has grown across the path. Field edges become quite a test of navigation; this applies to lower Swaledale and to the Vale of Mowbray in particular. By the end of a wet June the same paths are trampled mud.

EQUIPMENT AND SAFETY

It would be unwise to undertake this walk without experience of moorland or mountain walking, and indeed, bad-weather moorland or mountain walking. Walkers with such experience will make their own judgments on rucksack weight, speed of travel, acceptable discomfort and acceptable risk.

Walkers from abroad may appreciate some indication of English conditions. To them I suggest, between April and September, the three-layer clothing system (thermal, fleece and breathable waterproof) plus hat and gloves. Hillwalking boots should be lightweight, and could be fabric rather than leather. A compass should be carried: magnetic deviation is five degrees west. I take a survival bag or bivvy bag.

MAPS, WAYMARKING AND ACCESS

The Coast-to-Coast is not a National Trail and is not waymarked as such. The high ground is not way-marked at all: the lower ground follows public foot-paths, bridleways and permissive paths and is waymarked accordingly. Some specific C-to-C signs and waymarks have been erected: not all of these correspond with the version of the Coast-to-Coast offered in this, or any other, guidebook.

The route description and sketch-maps in this book are designed to get you across England without constant cross-reference to the map. However, even the most precise and lucid route-description is utterly useless if you happen not to be on the route. This could happen because of thick mist, alterations to the path, or even (Heaven forbid) because of ambiguity in the description itself. When you do go astray, it's essential to have a properly surveyed map to hand.

It is best to have a map with field edges marked. The OS Coast-to-Coast strip maps (Outdoor Leisure 33 and 34) are so convenient that it would be perverse not to use them, and I've assumed that readers are carrying them. They are at various points out-of-date, misleading or just wrong: I have pointed out some of these places in the text. A new edition is in preparation (partly as a result of a long letter from me!)

The OS maps cover a narrow strip, allowing little room for variant routes, seeking beds off-route, appreciating the wider geography or just plain getting lost. The two Coast-to-Coast maps by Footprint are small, cheap and convenient and cover a wider strip in less detail. They are a useful supplement to the OL strip-map and could, in particular, be carried by a member of the party who is not the main map reader. Those with orienteering-level compass skills could use them instead of the OL map.

Of the permitted routes over Nine Standards Rigg, only the August to November one is covered by the OL strip-map. The Footprint map covers also the spring route, and a map of all three routes (without contour detail) is obtainable, free, from Kirkby Stephen TI.

Harveys are intending to bring out a Coast-to-Coast strip map in the next year or two, and this, when it appears, will probably be more accurate than the OL map and also a great deal more waterproof.

For those wishing to venture into the hills and mountains alongside, the following six OS maps cover most of the route:

OL 27 North York Moors: East; OL 26 North York Moors: West; OL 30 Yorkshire Dales: North & Central; OL 19 Howgill Fells; OL 5 English Lakes: NE; OL 4 English Lakes: NW.

The two gaps can be covered by the strip-map, or by OS Landranger 89 (West Cumbria), OS Land-rangers 93, 99, 92 (Vale of Mowbray).

The Coast-to-Coast is not a right of way. You cannot assume that because a line is in this book, there is necessarily a permanent and absolute right to walk it. English landowners are on the whole a tolerant and hospitable lot, and Coast-to-Coast walkers have earned ourselves a reputation for courtesy and respect for the countryside; so it is unlikely that these permissions will be withdrawn.

If the route is diverted, it is almost certainly to allow footpaths to recover or be repaired. An alternative route will usually be indicated and waymarked.

HOW TO USE THIS GUIDE

Very occasionally I have given a compass bearing. In thick mist, a compass would be required at these points, although in clear weather all will usually be obvious. The descriptions are intended for a walker at the start of the season, when field paths are at their most inconspicuous. August walkers may feel I have an absurdly nervous attitude towards field-edge navigation!

Section 1:

Cumbria Coastal

Clifftops make a fine start to any walk, and the ones at St Bees are as good as any. It's a natural west end to Cumbria: it's 300ft (100m) high: it's gritty rusty-coloured sandstone with grass on top and it's covered in guillemots and razorbills. The crossing of the Cumbria Coastal Plain is one of those necessary linking bits – there's only five miles of it (8km) and at least you'll be doing it blisterless and fairly fresh. Muddy farm tracks run between hedges of hawthorn and gorse. After Bells Farm, a tricky stile-to-stile section requires close attention to route description and waymarks. In compensation, a mile and a half of railway line (2km) lets you put away the map and enjoy the sculptures.

It's possible to walk round Dent Fell: don't! Though no right of way, there's an established permissive path, and the moment you set foot on its slope you're in the hills, with no more 'linking bits' till Shap. Dent is a grassy top to lounge on, with half a horizon's-worth of sea behind, the white towers of Sellafield and the smoking chimneys of Whitehaven below; and ahead, a hundred Lakeland Hills. And down the back of Dent is Nannycatch: a sunken valley, walled with gorse and small crags, inhabited by hunting birds, people on ponies and walkers of the Coast-to-Coast.

DIFFICULTIES: The initial clifftop section is shelterless, and can be extremely windy, giving a foretaste of high mountain conditions to follow. The section between the active railway line and the abandoned one past Stanley Pond is field-edge navigation with little visible path. Forest roads at the back of Dent Fell, in Uldale Plantation, are not as they appear on the map.

ST BEES to ENNERDALE BRIDGE, 15 miles (24km): 2300ft (700m). GOING: easy, but moderate on field paths between the two railways.

St Bee – or Bega – was an Irish chieftain's daughter who wanted to be a nun not a wife so ran away to England: a real person, or at least, a real legend.

The walk starts at a sandstone display beyond the car park. Walk forward to the sea wall, then right along it to a metalwork bridge over the shingle. Many signposts point up the clifftop path, the only one not to follow being the one that says 'Rotting-ton'. 165 wooden steps mount to the first headland. A small concrete ruin gives a view back over the half-mile achieved, and forward to the lighthouse of St Bees Head.

The small dirt path runs outside the clifftop fence. After another mile (1.5 km) it drops into the sharp inlet of Fleswick, then crosses a steep slope out and up to regain the clifftop. Stiles on the left allow access to bird-watching stations on the very brink.

Apart from various seagulls, the birds to be seen here are guillemots (black and white, big beaks) and razorbills (browner, smaller, and with really enormous beaks). Every spring, 12,000 of the former and 2,000 of the latter nest on these cliffs – except that they don't actually nest, but simply choose a ledge that hasn't already got someone standing on it, that's not too deep in last year's

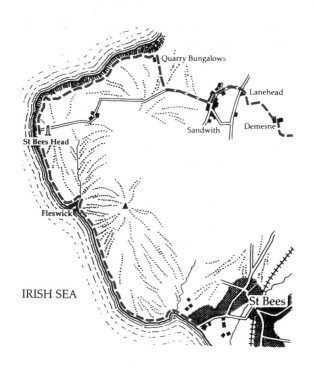

dung. If you fancy the life 'free as a bird' you may think again on contemplating the male guillemot, standing for three weeks on his crowded ledge, gazing out to sea with his egg between his feet. Those eggs are particularly pointed, to make them less likely to roll off the ledge.

A few jackdaws may swoop in acrobatic flight, and cormorants (or could they be shags?) stand on sea-level rocks in elegant long-necked poses, drying their wings in the wind.

ST BEES HEAD: Pass immediately inland of the small lookout hut, crossing the concrete track that leads up to the lighthouse. The clifftop path continues, sometimes just inside the clifftop fence, sometimes, excitingly, just outside it. After 1½ miles (2 km), the path skirts the rim of a quarry. (Gates here are from the Robin Hood Sawmill, Bassenthwaite: the first of many reminders of journey's eventual end.) Pass in front of the Quarry Bungalow, and turn right, into a track.

Almost at once the view of the sea behind is lost. (There is, rather disconcertingly, a view of the sea ahead; try to ignore that.) The track joins a tarred lane. Turn left and follow it for 600m/yds to Sandwith. Ahead are all the Lakeland fells, waiting for you to walk over them; low, forested Dent stands at the front of the queue.

SANDWITH: Turn left, and follow the main street past the Dog & Pheasant to a T-junction at Lanehead. Keep ahead on a track, tarred for its first 50m/yds, to the left of the house. The track continues as mud and grass between imposing hedges to Demesne Farm. Turn right between the buildings onto a stony track between hedges. This bends left to meet the main B5345. Just to the left is a sign 'Welcome to Whitehaven' – how closely we have escaped entering this town of smoking industry.

Go directly across onto the tarred driveway to Bell House. Pass to left of the buildings onto a track of reddish dirt that crosses a cattle grid. The track bends right, slanting downhill and forking: take the right-hand, upper track.

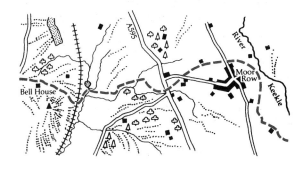

After 150m/yds, fork left on tractor wheelmarks. After 80m/yds these go through a gate, but turn off right in front of this gate and follow the hedge round to the bridge under the railway.

Once under the railway, slant left to join the fence along the far side of the field. Follow this to a way-marked stile on the right: Stanley Pond is immediately ahead, but all that can be seen is its fringe of reeds. Cross the stile, and follow the field edge on the left – this is at first a ditch, then a hedge, then a fence. At the field's end turn left through a way-marked field-gate, and follow a fence round to the right, passing a swampy pond.

Go up the field to a grey field-gate with stile alongside. Tractor ruts run out across another field to a muddy ford, with a sort of half-bridge alongside, and under the bridge of the disused railway. There will be no more tricky fieldwork till Shap (though it's also possible to get lost on the open fellside).

Go through under the bridge, and turn right through a stile of carved stone to the railbed above. Here turn left, and follow the tarred path, designed for walkers, cyclists and horseriders and equipped with benches and outdoor sculpture.

MOOR ROW: Pass under two road bridges to a third. Now, to visit the shop in Moor Row, turn right on the road overhead. Otherwise continue ahead to a junction of tarred paths. Here turn right (waymark, 'Alternative Coast-to-Coast') and in 10m/yds, ahead (rather than right again on a path into Moor Row).

The trackbed goes over the sunken Blind Lane, and under two bridges. In another 250m/yds, an untarred path forks off left (no sign or waymark). This joins the end of a tarred lane beside a cricket pitch. The lane bends left, to cross a stream within sniffing distance of the sewage works, onto the main street of CLEATOR.

Turn left on the main street, and in 20m/yds right into Kiln Brow – the house at the turning has its front door inset into the corner of the building. After 100m/yds a sign points right 'Fell Road via Nook Farm'. This street crosses the River Ehen, and immediately turns left to become what is either a very rough road or a very smooth track between thorn hedges. This leads by way of three right-angle bends into the mud and slurry at the back of Black How Farm.

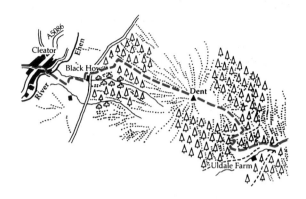

Turn right just after the farm as the track reverts to earth (C-to-C sign), and cross the road in front. A wide gate leads onto a forest road that slants uphill. After 400m/yds, a C-to-C sign points left. The path runs forward for 60m/yds, then turns right, uphill, at another sign (C-to-C, Dent). A wide ride with narrow path leads uphill, with first an earthen bank on the right, and later a broken wall. A gateway leads out onto the open hillside. A bench is just above; on this bench sits, as likely as not, a Coast-to-Coast walker with his boots off.

The broken wall on the right marks the way up the grassy slope.

DENT FELL: The first, western summit has the cairn and is the better viewpoint. Follow the broken wall towards the eastern and higher one. A morass lies in the col between the two: eastbound walkers, each lifting a stone from the ruined wall, are gradually dropping a causeway across it. From the true summit the descent is south-east, on a bearing of 120 degrees and an indistinct path, to a stile in the fence at the top of the trees. (The plantation top is at the 330m contour, higher than on the OL map.)

A wet ride leads down between the trees on the same bearing to a five-way junction. Turn sharp right, to pass two galvanised tanks among the trees. Diagonally across a forest road is the top of a neglected track that zigzags down, finally to meet another forest road above Uldale Farm. Turn left for 300m/yds, and after crossing a bridge, head up beside the little stream of NANNYCATCH.

A wide, smooth path, used by horseriders, runs up this tight little valley. After half a mile (800m), the valley runs below the grey turrets of Raven Crag. Here is seen for the first time the rough volcanic rock of Lakeland; and here the valley forks. The Coast-to-Coast takes the right branch.

After another ³/₄ mile (1 km) the valley forks again. Again, take the right branch. After 200m/yds the stream, now very small, turns right, up the side wall. The right of way leaves the horse-path, and goes up with the stream to the moor road just above. Turn left along the road, which passes the stone circle of Blakeley Moor after a few yards. The stones were placed in the 19th century as an example of an archaeological remain – a real Stone-Ager would never have placed two odd ones of the pinkish Ennerdale Granophyre among the grey Borrowdale Volcanic.

The road crosses a cattle grid – here a parish footpath is proposed that may one day turn off left for a nicer approach to Ennerdale Bridge. For the time being, there's only the road, which slithers downhill for a mile (1.5 km). At the junction with the larger valley road, the signpost points right for Ennerdale Bridge. The attractive village is even more attractive as it probably offers the first night's harbourage, and is reached in another 500m/yds.

Section 2:
Ennerdale

Most of us enter and leave Lakeland by car. The Coast-to-Coast enters and leaves Lakeland by lake. The moment round the foot of Angler's Crag can be, with a cumbersome backpack, a little bit exciting. But then it's all straightforward pleasure: a path over tree roots, high craggy slopes, and the sun (or, alternatively, the rain) beating down onto the water and trickling its way among the leaves.

You'll see three pretty valleys later. The bottom part of Ennerdale's a wood-pulp factory, and the top's a bowl of hummocks, with grey clouds at the rim in which lurk Gable, Pillar and Kirkfell. The attraction of Ennerdale is of a place without a road, that is nonetheless a busy highway where walkers from St Bees meet cyclists circling their seven valleys, and where there are two youth hostels that can't be reached by car.

It's just a shame about those four miles of forestry plantation. However, the streamside path is pleasant enough, and after that there's an option to rise out of the trees onto the screes. Hay Stacks is small but splendid: a bite-size chunk of Lakeland rocky mountain, two tarns and some dodging among the rocks.

The crossing to Honister is somewhat industrialised: remnants of the slate industry, and a tarred car park at 1,100ft (330m). The next three passes will be better.

DIFFICULTIES: The main route has two tiresome miles of forest road (3km); the climb up Loft Beck is

short but very steep, and eroded. The path round the head of Dubs Bottom is not well-marked, and the contours are confusing: in mist, this will require full hill skills. The Hay Stacks alternative involves rough rocky ground. In mist it is even more confusing than the main route by Loft Beck, and has crags to fall over if you go wrong.

ENNERDALE BRIDGE to HONISTER, 12 miles (19km): 1900ft (550m). GOING: easy to head of

Ennerdale, then hard ascent of Loft Beck and moderate (rough path) to Honister. Hay Stacks alternative: 12 miles (19km): 2300ft (700m)

Take the tarred road up-valley (signpost 'Ennerdale Water') and fork right at sign 'Ennerdale Lake 1' – there's no such place, of course, it's still Ennerdale Water they mean. After 500m/yds the road bends left, and here a track leads ahead past Grike Cottage. At the track's end, cross a stile to right of the Mill, to a long and bouncy footbridge over the Ehen.

A green track crosses a stile, and runs up to a forest road. Turn left, along the bottom of the trees. At the track end above Crag Farm, ease down left to the wall just below. A small path runs along the upper side of this wall, and leads round to the lakeside.

Many walkers, of course, have been before us between Ennerdale and St Bees: but also one beast, the tiger-striped, big-jawed, monster dog of Ennerdale. During the spring and summer of 1810, this animal spent its nights attacking sheep, and its days leading the people of Ennerdale on fruitless long-distance pursuits. It chanced to pass during Sunday service and emptied the church, the vicar pausing only to extinguish the altar candles before joining in a chase that led halfway to Cockermouth. The outing from Ennerdale Bridge to St Bees was one of the shorter day-walks for the animal and pursuing people. The animal hid in a garden near the priory, leaving the people to make their own way back to Ennerdale.

Come autumn, the harvesting of the crops deprived the 'Girt Beast' of cover, and it was shot at the end of Septem-

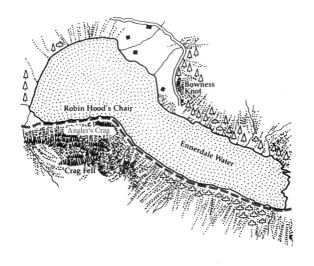

ber by one John Steel. Steel got a ten pound reward, while the dog was stuffed and presented to the museum at Keswick. The carcass weighed in at 8 stones (50 kg).

The next four miles along the south side of Ennerdale Water are along a small path with a big, big view of the major mountains up valley. First it passes below the shaky-looking pinnacles of Revelin Crag, and then a rock-backed patch of grass at the waterside known as Robin Hood's Chair. (Clearly, then, he thought nothing of walking here from his Bay in the east, simply for a pipe and a read of the newspaper after his tea.)

Now Anglers' Crag drops steeply into the water. The path clambers through its lower rocks. Where there is a choice of paths, the higher one involves

some loose scree, awkward with a heavy rucksack. Disentangling itself from the rocks, the path crosses the top of a plunging pink scree; the line of the slope can be seen continuing beneath the waterline.

Slightly rough but enjoyable walking leads to a footbridge at the head of the Water. A broad grassy path leads to the left of a forestry plantation, over stile and then ladder stile, to a forest road. Turn right through a complex triple gate and left on the road just inside the forest. After 100m/yds, green-topped waymarks on the left indicate the way to the Liza footbridge for those wanting Gillerthwaite Youth Hostel. Otherwise, continue ahead (sign 'Liza Beck Path') to the bridge over the Woundell Beck.

After 200m/yds the track bends right, and green waymarks lead ahead. The path runs along the forest edge, next to the open ground beside the river.

After ³/₄ mile (1 km), it joins a green forest track beside the Moss Dub pool. In 100m/yds, the path branches back off to the left, crossing two footbridges to the riverbank. It stays beside the river, and after crossing the High Beck, is waymarked in both blue and green. After another 800m/yds, it runs onto a forest road.

At the time of writing, the Liza Beck path ahead is merely an idea, two odd waymarks and a lot of brushwood. (If visible signs of path have appeared, continue on this bank: for those wanting Hay Stacks, there's a footbridge in 1000m/yds.) So turn left over the river, and right on the main forest road beyond.

The ground above is now clear-felled, allowing views up to the High Stile ridge. 50m/yds before the end of the clear-fell, and just after a side-path on the right to a footbridge, a path signed 'Scarth Gap' slants up left. This is taken by those who want to enjoy the Hay Stacks alternative route (described at the end of the section).

The rest of us continue along the road for another mile (1.5 km). Where it bends right at the end of the trees, a rough track leads through a gate into the open air. This leads to the BLACK SAIL HUT.

The track passes along the front of the youth hostel, and down to the footbridge over the Liza. Do not cross, but continue up the north bank for 800m/yds to a stream junction. Cross the left stream (Loft Beck), and follow it up into the deep slot in the valley side. As the ground steepens, a path forms, and as it steepens further, the path becomes an eroded horror. It's a fine place, with walls of stones and heather, but an unpleasant struggle either uphill or down.

Pass this way at the end of May or in mid-June, and you may meet a man with a hunting horn who wears a tattered sash. He is taking part in a hundred-year-old sport that happens here and nowhere else on Earth: the Lakes Hunt. The rules are those of the children's game of catch, the man in the sash is the quarry, and the territory extends along the Coast-to-Coast between Black Sail and Seatoller, while on either hand it reaches Wasdale Head and Winscale Bottom by Buttermere.

It's an exhausting and somewhat dangerous sport: high-speed chases often take place down Loft Beck, as well as over the cloudy boulders of Gable, the screes of Hay Stacks and the quarry workings of Fleetwith Pike. So if a man in a sash pretends to be part of your party, don't give him away – you may see some interesting sport.

As the ground eases onto the grassy plateau, a faint path leads forward, but if in mist or any doubt, confirm it with a compass-bearing (70 degrees). After 300m/yds the way passes through the remains of an iron fence, and then bends gradually left round the head of Dubs Bottom, to run into a larger path descending from above.

This larger path, with cairns, descends northwards, to join the tramway path at its highest point, where it is raised on an embankment. Ascend onto the tramway, and turn right. It descends arrow-straight towards Honister Hause, but as it steepens, an erosion fence crosses it, and walkers are diverted onto

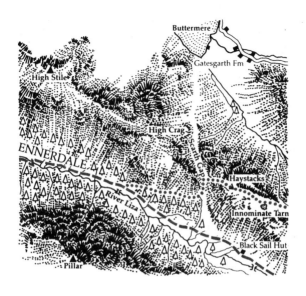

a newly-built path to the left. This bends back to rejoin the tramway, and after a few yards the tramway joins a lower track at a large cairn (the cairn is collecting money for the Cockermouth Rescue Team).

Follow the track east for 100m/yds: before the quarry buildings, a gate leads out to the tarred road and the youth hostel.

HAY STACKS VARIANT

It's tempting to call this the 'High-level' variant: but the summit of Hay Stacks is 3m (10ft) lower than the high point of the easier, Loft Beck route. However, Hay Stacks

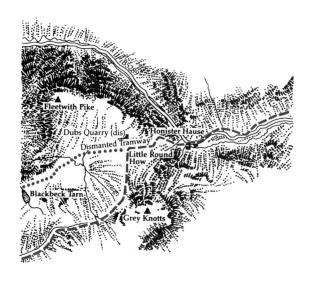

*is a big mountain in everything but height, and makes a
nice pair with the equally rocky Helm Crag (which may
be wandered out onto in the following section). In clear
weather, it adds just half an hour to the route. In nasty
weather, it could subtract the rest of your life... that's if
you managed to wander over the crags above Buttermere.*

The path for Scarth Gap leaves the forest road
under High Crag, just before the end of the clear-
felled area. It passes through a corner of the forest,
enters and leaves a high clear-felled area at stiles,
and slants up into Scarth Gap.

A newly-built path leads up the craggy end of Hay
Stacks. After the first rise it wanders left – a more
direct route is nicer, with some easy scrambling up

a rock-tier. A small tarn lies before HAY STACKS SUMMIT, which has a cairn on the left.

A wide path makes its way down among knolls to pass to the left of Innominate Tarn. Lakeland tarns are ridgetop, moorland or corrie. This is a lovely example of the ridgetop variety, set among rocks and craglets, with a view of wide sky and the tops of surrounding mountains. Here are scattered the ashes of Alfred Wainwright, originator of the Coast-to-Coast Walk.

From the tarn the path descends without change of direction, to cross the top of a cragged slope over-looking the length of Buttermere, and reach the outflow of the Blackbeck Tarn. It continues up the short slope opposite, then passes to right of the rock summit of Green Crag. It goes immediately left of the rock-knoll of Little Round How and drops to the boggy flat ground of Dubs Bottom.

Across the stream, the path leads off left towards Buttermere, so keep ahead up the slope into quarry workings. At a slate building is the start of the straight path climbing gently to the right: the old tramway. Follow this up for 600m/yds onto its embankment, and down the backslope to Honister Hause.

Section 3:

Central Fells

"A truly secreted spot is this, completely surrounded by the most horrid romantic mountains," thus was Borrowdale in West's Guide of 1774. West was a brave man: earlier guidebooks had turned back in terror at Grange. Few today are frightened of Borrowdale, which is generally considered the loveliest in the Lakes – and so, presumably, the most beautiful spot in England. (It is, by a more certain measure, the wettest.) Lumpy hillsides with rock breaking out all over; deep vigorous woodlands; a flat fertile valley floor, criss-crossed with stone walls; and, splashing down the sides and curving across the fertile floor, the water from all that rainfall.

The pass across the Central Fells is high and remote – a route unsuspected from either end. It starts to go up Langstrath, but then makes its oblique way around the flank of Ullscarf. The bog at the head of Wythburn is a place apart, ringed by crags and peaks. In this high world, pints of beer and dry socks are distant dreams merely.

The choice at Easedale Head is between the high-level route over Helm Crag, and the descent into Far Easedale. Far Easedale is more logical, turning this stage of the walk into a complex high pass between two valley heads. Far Easedale is also far easier! Many will choose it for one or other of these reasons; but Easedale is also an extremely pretty Lakeland valley, with crags, waterfalls, and a streamside path leading gently to the wooded lower section.

However, the ridge over Gibson Knott is a knolly ramble,

and the summit of Helm Crag is a sculptural and over-hanging crag. Those who fancy the scramble to one of Lakeland's two hands-on summits will choose the Helm Crag route. (The other hands-on summit? The awe-inspiring Pillar Rock. Rather than awe, Helm Crag inspires affection.)

DIFFICULTIES:

A short field-edge section into Rosthwaite is indifferently waymarked.

The pass from Borrowdale to Grasmere is a serious hill crossing. The path is unwaymarked, lightly cairned, and not always distinct. In mist, it will require careful attention to the compass and to the lie of the ground. The path, assuming you've stayed on it, is rough and in places boggy. The first part of the high-level option, past Calf Crag, is similarly boggy and confusing.

HONISTER HAUSE TO GRASMERE, 10½ miles (17km): 1800ft (550m). GOING: hard. Including Helm Crag: 11 miles (18km): 2200ft (650m)

Go down the motor road for 400m/yds, then branch off left on wet path that is, in fact, the old road down the pass. After 300m/yds it rejoins the road for 50m/yds, then branches off again left, now a stony track. The new road is at first just below, but soon it plunges away with a crashing of gearboxes in a steep descent along the river. Our track drops more gently, getting a fine view down Borrowdale before turning sharply back right towards Seatoller.

For a shortcut that misses out Seatoller, drop from the old road at this bend, going steeply down a grass path and crossing the stream on the left to the wall below. The exit path from Seatoller runs alongside the wall, and a few steps left will reach the kissing gate into the wood below.

SEATOLLER: Turn left down the road, ignoring the farm entrance track on the left and passing Seatoller House, the rallying-point and residence of the Lakes Hunt. On the left is a small car park (footpath sign 'Johnny Wood'). From the back of the car park a short track leads up to a gate and stile.

After the stile, turn right along the wall (do not continue uphill on the track). After 150m/yds this path descends through the wall at a kissing gate into a wood. Above Folly Bridge the path bears slightly left through an ungated gap, to pass along the bottom edge of open field and enter the bottom of Johnny Wood: this is the first really nice woodland of the walk, though there are many more to look forward to. It is supposed to be a remnant of the post ice-age tree cover.

The path soon reaches the river, where it is forced to cross waterworn bare rock. After another 100m/yds it passes along the front of Longthwaite Youth Hostel. (From the foot of Ennerdale Water the Coast-to-Coast has passed just four habitations: all four have been youth hostels!)

At the hostel's entrance gates bear right across Longthwaite Bridge. In 50m/yds the tarred lane turns right: here a footpath sign points left along a gravel path with a cottage to left. Cross a stile, and

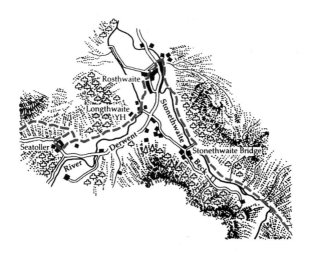

go forward with wall and fence to right to a way-marked gate on the right. Cross the field corner to a stile, and go forward with a wall on your right.

With the back gardens of Rosthwaite on the other side of the wall, the path is now clear. It crosses through a gap in the rock bar that formerly held in the Lake Stonethwaite (one of four that once filled the floor of Borrowdale). After a field gate turn right, onto the lane that leads left into Rosthwaite.

At a non-existent point close to the Hazel Bank Hotel stands Herries, the setting for Hugh Walpole's Borrowdale novels. 'Rogue Herries', 'Judith Paris', 'The Fortress' and 'Vanessa' are high romance, with a sultry maiden on the cover and a family tree on page 10. They tell the fortunes of the Herries family from 1730 to the 1930's, when the books themselves were written. But the real hero of the stories is Borrowdale, as in this description, from 'Rogue Herries', of the valley's rainfall:

"It was rain of a relentless, determined, soaking, penetrating kind. No other rain anywhere, at least in the British Isles (which has a prerogative of many sorts of rain), falls with so determined a fanatic obstinacy as does this rain. It is not that the sky in any deliberate mood decides to empty itself. It is rain that has but little connection either with earth or sky, but rather has a life of its own, stern, remorseless and kindly. It falls in sheets of steely straightness, and through it is the rhythm of the beating hammer. It is made up of opposites, impersonal and yet greatly personal, strong and gentle, ironical and understanding. The one thing that it is not is sentimental."

ROSTHWAITE

Take the main Keswick road down-valley, and at the edge of the village turn right over a stone arch (sign 'Bridleway Stonethwaite'). A second sign ('By-Way Stonethwaite') points to the right.

The way is a stony path between high walls, first through the riverbank trees and then below fields. The Stonethwaite Beck is on the right, and beyond it the steep face of Bessyboot, clothed luxuriously in oak. After 1½ miles (2.5 km) the track becomes path, and the valley forks. To right is the long level valley of Langstrath: the path that crosses a wooden footbridge down right is Langstrath's path, and part of the Cumbria Way, but our way is ahead, up the steepening side-valley of Greenup Gill.

This left-hand path immediately starts to climb,

with the stream below on the right. On the right-hand side of the valley, high Eagle Crag is clearly overhanging. Ahead is the triangular buttress of Lining Crag. After a stretch among grassy moraine-knolls, the path climbs steeply, close up against this crag and to left of it. This section has been rebuilt as pitched path. According to Naismith's formula, the 500 feet of ascent should be considered as an extra 3/4 mile (or the 150m as an extra 1.2 km). If the steep climb is taken as slowly as this calculation would imply, it will not prove too arduous.

The path emerges suddenly onto the flat grassy spur that is the top of the crag. It continues gently

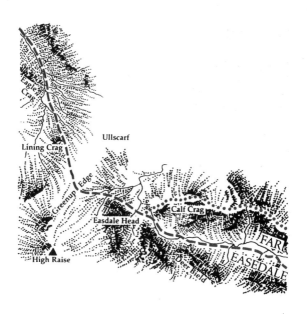

uphill, with only occasional cairns and slightly more frequent boggy bits, becoming indistinct as it approaches the col. In mist it is easy to go astray here. Two things may help: a compass bearing (170 degrees), and the scattered remnants of old iron fence that run down into the col from both sides.

Note that GREENUP EDGE is the first col of what is a double pass. A direct descent from here would take you down the Wythburn Valley, and a second col will have to be crossed to reach Easedale.

The col has several cairns, including two marking the clear onward path that goes straight down the far side. After five minutes of descent, the path crosses the stream of Flour Gill and slants down to right – a smaller path, going straight on down Wythburn, is used by those attempting the Lakeland Threethousanders on their way to Helvellyn (and also, not infrequently, by lost Coast-to-Coast walkers).

The path levels off, without change of direction, and crosses flat boggy ground below the crag of Birks. A short rise leads to the col at the head of Easedale. Here a ridge-path crosses, as well as a derelict iron fence. The place has a cairn, and also a pair of posts forming a gateway in the fallen fence.

Here is the turnoff for Helm Crag. That high-level route is described at the end of the section.

EASEDALE HEAD: From the col, take the path straight ahead. This is peaty at first, but becomes clear as it descends to join the stream. It descends alongside it for 200ft/60m vertical, then turns right to cross it. Here is one of the most attractive resting-places of the walk. Behind is a spreading waterfall on a side-beck, while the other stream has just emerged from a ferny gorge. Just above is a small lawn to eat sandwiches on.

The path continues down steeply to the valley floor. The remaining two miles (3km) to Grasmere are a gentle stroll along the quiet and very attractive valley. Above is the steep slitted crag of Deer Bield. (The deep hole in the right is Deer Bield Chimney, the crack on the left is Deer Bield Crack, and from the final pitch of the Chimney you can look right through and see rather better rock-climbers struggling with the final pitch of the Crack.)

The path crosses to the stream's left bank by a long footbridge. Trees overhang the grassy bank. On the left is a striking roche moutonnée or 'sheepified rock' worn rounded by glacier. Here the path dives down into a rock-floored gully. After another 300m/yds the Helm Crag variant route rejoins at a three-way signpost.

LANCRIGG WOOD: From the signpost where the alternative routes rejoin, take the eastward track (Grasmere) for 100m/yds to go through a gate. The track ahead, floored with slate stones jammed edgewise, leads to Easedale Road and Grasmere, but feet are tempted by a small gate on the left. This leads up steps into Lancrigg Wood (sign 'permissive path: through route to Grasmere').

The path climbs slightly through the wood: ignore a descending right fork after 100m/yds. You pass a small Wordsworth Memorial – this one, unusually and pleasingly, is to Dorothy, she who willingly gave him many of the best ideas for his poems, and then stood back and told everyone how wonderful he was.

HOC IN SUPERCILIO SEDEBAT DOROTHEA WORDSWORTH DUM EX ORE FRATRIS PROPE INAMBULANTIS CARMINA DESCRIBIT

'Here on a hummock sat Dorothy Wordsworth while from the mouth of her brother wandering nearby she transcribed verses.'

Thus Wordsworth is conveniently incorporated into the walk; this saves you having to hurry to catch Dove Cottage before it closes.

In 50m/yds the path goes through a gate and descends to pass along the front of the Lancrigg Hotel. And if the hotel has laid the permissive path partly with the intention of entrapping hungry walkers, why should hungry walkers complain?

Turn right (or left, a shortcut to Thorny How) down the hotel's driveway to join Easedale Road. Follow the lane downhill. The first turning left, signposted to Thorny How Youth Hostel, will be the exit from Grasmere. A dog-walking path on the right lets you escape the tarmac briefly, as the street becomes busy with walkers' cars. It passes the other, Butter-lips How, youth hostel, to emerge onto the main square of Grasmere.

HELM CRAG VARIANT

On reaching the col at Easedale Head turn left, on a path that initially traverses the top of the steep Easedale slope. Ascend gradually to the rock-knoll of Calf Crag – the path passes just to left of its small cairn. Follow the path due east round the rim of Easedale until it descends, without change of direction, onto the Gibson's Knott ridge.

The going is now much drier. The path follows the ridge, or traverses on right-hand slopes above Easedale. Several knolls make up the imprecise hill of Gibson's Knott – the final knoll has the cairn on, and the path passes just below it on the right, then traverses below a small crag on the Easedale flank and drops into the col before Helm Crag. Go straight up to the summit.

> *'Here see, raised up to human view*
> *The kingly Lion and his victims two.*
> *I see but one! the wanderer cried.*
> *That's right: the other one's inside'*

So ran the verse my granny taught me. In the context of its time, a slightly naughty rhyme: for the Lion and the Lamb come out of the book of Isaiah. At the coming of the Messiah: "the wolf also shall dwell with the lamb, and the leopard shall lie down with the kid; and the calf and the young lion and the fatling together; and a little child shall lead them. They shall not hurt, nor destroy, in all My holy mountain."

The summit rocks of Helm Crag resemble the lion and the lamb – but which summit rocks? From Dunmail Raise it is the northern, more difficult, top that resembles the two designated animals: from Grasmere it's the lesser, southern summit. So two lions, two lambs – or, counting the ones already devoured, two lions, four lambs.

HELM CRAG: The rocks of the northern, higher summit overhang impressively on the Dunmail side, but are steep around the base even on the 'easy' side. The scramble to the very top is tougher than you'd expect on such a friendly little hill. The easiest way starts at the west corner, and grabs large handholds into the obvious gap behind a pinnacle. Traverse right, across a slab, then slant up right below the summit.

The trig point marked on the lower summit doesn't exist. Descend the east ridge until you're about to drop off the end down the chimneys of Grasmere. The path then turns right to zigzag down the Easedale flank to a gate at the bottom of the woods. Go down the track beyond for 100m/yds to a track junction with signpost left for Grasmere, to rejoin the Far Easedale route (Lancrigg Wood).

Section 4:

Grisedale Hause

The third high crossing is a pass in the classic style. From the very bottom you look up to the very top: the high gap that's the way through between higher mountains. Or else you don't – if it happens to be misty. In low cloud Grisedale Hause is even better, with dark shadows of crag on either hand, and the sheltered tarn a place of real sanctuary. Most walkers here climb high stony mountains on sunny days. They do not know the drama of the high pass in the storm.

Still, if the sun should be shining, then high mountains are the thing to do. Under clear skies, look east to ST SUNDAY CRAG. The ascent to Deepdale Hause dodges delightfully among the outcrops, and is followed by a genuine ridge-walk where you can look down two steep sides at once. The descent traverses long and gently above the deep hole of Grisedale. If the final descent of Thornhow End is unpleasantly steep, this gives excuse for several stops to contemplate Ullswater.

For the less ambitious, the tired, or the tempest-tossed, the simple descent is straight down GRISEDALE. After a steep start, Grisedale is sheltered and gentle.

DIFFICULTIES:

GRISEDALE VARIANT is steep in places, on the way up and on the way down. However, the steep sections are rebuilt pitched path.

ST SUNDAY CRAG is a serious hill: in mist, the

route off the top is not clear, and there are crags alongside. The final descent of Thornhow End is steep and eroded.

GRASMERE TO PATTERDALE, 9½ miles (16 km): 1,800ft (550m). GOING: easy/moderate. ST SUNDAY CRAG Variant: 9½ miles (16km): 2,800ft (850m)

Leave the village by Easedale Road, and after 600m/yds turn right at a sign 'Thorny How Youth Hostel'. At the next junction, turn right over the River Rothay to reach the main A591 (Dunmail Raise) road 200m/yds north of the Travellers' Rest.

Cross the busy road to a walled track opposite (sign 'Patterdale'). This goes uphill to a gate after 100m/yds, and then above the small gorge of Tonguegill Force – you look down on treetops, the noisy waterfalls are out of sight below the leaves. The track climbs to another gate just before the junction of streams (Tongue Gill, Little Tongue Gill).

There is now a choice of routes: Little Tongue Gill (left) or Tongue Gill (right). The Little Tongue Gill route is pleasanter, with a grassy path and a traverse below the rocks of Gavel Crag. In mist, though, there are route-finding difficulties at the head of the stream and the TONGUE GILL route is more straightforward.

For this easier route, turn down right at the stream junction, to a footbridge overhung by willows. The clear and well-built path is gentle at first along the valley side. At the combe head it crosses left below

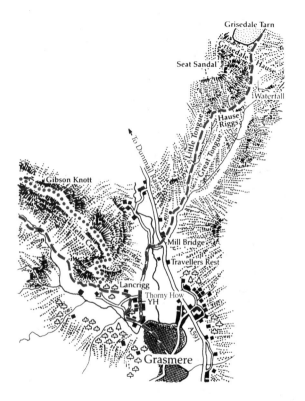

waterfalls, climbing steeply on a pitched path till it eases into the rocky upper combe.

LITTLE TONGUE GILL: At the stream junction stay on the track ahead as it fords the left-hand stream – stepping stones are beside the ford. The grassy track goes up the little stream valley, with the stream on its left, then crosses it. Now take a path uphill to right of the stream: the path starts stony, then becomes a grassy band through the bracken.

At the top of the stream, paths tend off right; but ignore them, continuing uphill to pass the left-hand corner of a small rock outcrop (Hause Riggs). Turn right, along the top of the outcrop. A clear path traverses quite steep and rocky ground, with crags above and views out to Grasmere. It bends round the hillside to join the pitched path that is the alternative Tongue Gill route.

Turn uphill on this steep path, which eases as it enters the upper combe (Hause Moss). Here is a remote and gloomy place, as befits the achievement of a high pass. Crags of Seat Sandal overhang it, and the combe floor is decorated with fallen boulders. Boggy ground on the right is the remains of a former tarn. The path steepens again for a final section of pitched path to the col.

Turn right at the pass, and drop gradually to the outflow of Grisedale Tarn.

Of the ancient Celtic kingdom of Cumberland there remains only the occasional Gaelic place-name, such as Glenridding. The reason why Cumbrians now favour wrestling and hound trails rather than eisteddfods and rugby football is the battle of Dunmail Rise (944). The last Celtic king of Cumberland, Dunmail, was mortally wounded in the battle; the victor, Edmund of England, passed the country into the care of Malcolm of Scotland; the Celtic inhabitants emigrated en masse to Snowdonia.

One legend has Dunmail under the pile of stones beside

the dual carriageway, but according to another he fled the battlefield by way of Stake Beck towards Patterdale; and, realising that the kingdom was at an end, hurled the crown of Cumberland into the grey waters of Grisedale Tarn. Note that this is a particularly unreliable legend: that Grisedale Tarn is 115 feet deep (35m) and very cold: and that any gold spiky objects you may discover are treasure trove and belong to the Queen of England.

However long we linger beside the tarn, we must eventually decide whether we shall now sink gently into Grisedale, or rise to the challenge of St Sunday Crag. The high-mountain route is described at the end of the section.

GRISEDALE ROUTE

Stay on the main path, to cross the tarn's outflow on wobbly stones. After 50m/yds, a large cairn marks where the path for Helvellyn turns back left; here keep ahead.

The path descends the left side of Grisedale, over bare rock in places. Below the climbers' hut of Ruthwaite Lodge is a steep descent, and then the path divides. The forward branch, which is for Glenridding, at once crosses a footbridge. The path we want, for Patterdale, turns off right, and after 150m/yds crosses a footbridge of its own. This one, across the Grisedale Beck, has a rowan tree growing out from below its footway.

The path continues down the right-hand side of the valley, eventually becoming a walled track with gates. Below Thornhow End it runs into the corner of a tarred lane. Go forward along the lane for 400m/yds. A footpath sign on the right indicates a stony track uphill, to a stile at the bottom of a wood. Above the stile, we turn left as we rejoin the route descending off St Sunday Crag.

THORNHOW END: The two routes now recombined follow the wide path south-east across the foot of Thornhow End, to cross Hag Beck on stepping-stones. The path continues on the same level, as a stone wall joins it from below. At a cross-wall, go forward through a kissing-gate and downhill with the wall on the left.

The path runs down a series of rocky knolls to a kissing gate into a birchwood. Just inside the wood, it forks. The left branch leads to the car park of the Patterdale Hotel; the right branch leads to the village shop and the track for Boredale Hause, Haweswater and (eventually) Robin Hood's Bay.

ST SUNDAY CRAG alternative

GRISEDALE TARN

Do not cross the outflow, but head east on a very small path that becomes obscure as it crosses boggy ground at the foot of the slope. After 100m/yds the path becomes plain as it starts to slant up the rocky slope towards Deepdale Hause. This path is delightful, passing behind rocky knolls and often taking a few steps downward to avoid some obstacle. It reaches the col at its eastern end, at the base of St Sunday's south-west ridge.

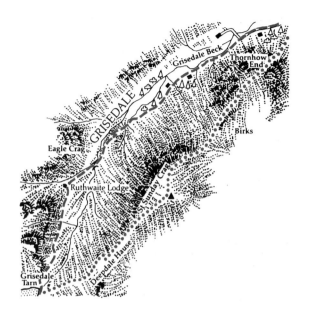

This ridge is wide and grassy – it's a walk, not a scramble – but steep sides drop to Grisedale and to Deepdale. The summit of ST SUNDAY CRAG is reached all too soon. The descent starts as a wide gravelly ridge, with no visible path; the few sprawling cairns are little help in mist and a compass bearing will be required (due north). The ridge then narrows, for a steep and stony descent. After the first col it slants down to the left along the slope of Birks, descending more steeply after passing through a broken wall.

The slope becomes broken and rocky, and the final traverse out to the nose of Thornhow End is on a narrow path above a drop into Grisedale. Views ahead along Ullswater are outstanding. The path reaches the point of the spur at a stone wall, and then descends through scattered oaks. At the bottom it reaches a fence with stile: do not cross the stile, but turn right to continue as on the valley route (THORNHOW END).

Section 5:

Patterdale to Shap

This is the highest crossing, and also the hardest.

The logic of the long-distance walk is to take the natural way between difficulties, and in this context the summit of Kidsty Pike (2,574ft old height, now slightly lower at 781m) is a necessary obstacle on the descent route. What doesn't make sense is to go out sideways and start walking all over the difficulties. However, the Roman road does lead along to High Street by way of a narrow edge above Riggindale, and the descent of LONG STILE, though without difficulty, is sharper and sweeter than that shoulder of Kidsty.

The end of the mountain ground may bring relief; from here on, hills will be lower and less steep, and the next proper bog is thirty miles (50km) away. However, it may also bring regrets. There will be no more great crags, and bare rock of any sort will be an occasional treat. Water will be something you buy from a shop. Perhaps it really would have been better backwards, with Lakeland at the end... Activity dispels doubt, and within a couple of steps of the end of Naddle Wood we're engaged in complex field studies with map and route plan. Such intellectual pursuits will be part of every day from now on.

The crossing of Knott and Kidsty is above 2,000 feet for more than 3 miles (above 600m for 5km). Walkers have been turned back by snow even in May, and by foul weather at any time. The ground around Knott can be particularly confusing with cold hands and wet map in a blizzard. For some, this just adds to the fun. For the rest of us, the less exposed ULLSWATER route is offered. The gain is the Ullswater lakeside. Haweswater, Ennerdale are good, but the Ullswater path is much better than that. The variant is four miles longer, but has 1,500 ft less ascent (6km longer, 450m less climb). The day may be shortened by seeking accommodation at Bampton.

DIFFICULTIES:

Main Route (KIDSTY PIKE): High exposed crossing with serious navigational difficulties in mist. Intricate field navigation leading to Shap Abbey.

ULLSWATER VARIANT: little-used paths from Moor Divock onward require careful navigation.

PATTERDALE to SHAP, 14 miles (22.5km): 3,200ft (950m). GOING: hard. ULLSWATER Variant: 18 miles (29km): 1,700ft (500m). GOING: easy-moderate.

Leave the village at its eastern end, and take a tarred lane left that immediately crosses Goldrill Beck on a bridge with criss-cross metal sides. Across the valley floor, the lane bends left to a gate on the right. Signs are for Boredale Hause. The path heads up to the right and, after only 200m/yds, divides. The two branches run up the hill in parallel and seem to be going to the same place – but they aren't. The lower one must be taken, and the upper one, past the iron bench, ignored.

It's often said that people who reach Patterdale don't want to leave. This is particularly so if the path they have to leave by is this steep and rather

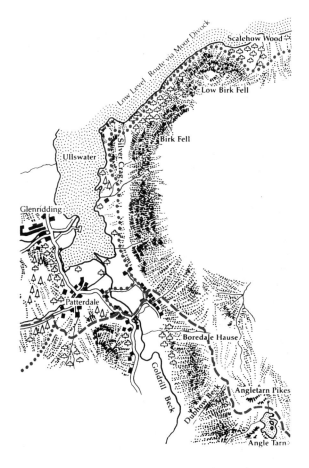

Scalehow Wood

Low Level Route via Moor Divock

Low Birk Fell

Birk Fell

Ullswater

Silver Crag

Glenridding

Patterdale

Boredale Hause

Goldrill Beck

Dubhow Beck

Angletarn Pikes

Angle Tarn

eroded one. The harsh ascent ends at the com-
plicated junction that is Boredale Hause. Here, at a
level green patch with cairn, five paths meet. Take
the one ahead (140 degrees) passing a stone enclo-

sure just down to the right and crossing a stream (Stonebarrow Gill) just 30m/yds from the junction.

After 200m/yds the path rejoins the same stream, to go up alongside it in its narrow re-entrant. The path emerges onto open fellside at the head of Dubhow Beck, with a sudden view down to the Kirkstone road; and here it divides.

The lower path traverses the top of a high, steep slope above the Kirkstone Pass: one of the nicest miles of the walk. However, the path is narrow and a slip could be a long one. On days of wind or snow, in particular, the higher, left-hand path is advised. Each path arrives suddenly above Angle Tarn, where they rejoin.

ANGLE TARN

Those using the OS strip-map will find the following section confusing. The way will follow the pink dots as far as the crossing of the broken wall south of Rest Dodd: then the pecked line (footpath) to join the yellow-striped right of way. The clear side-path to Hartsop is not where this map shows it.

The path curves round above the north shore of the tarn, and touches the ridge-crest for a brief look down Bannerdale; then traverses to right of the ridge to a gate. It continues with a wall on its right, but leaves this to wander off to the left, in a rather spineless attempt to avoid the final contour ring of the summit of Satura Crag. It bends back right to rejoin the wall, which at this point becomes a fence.

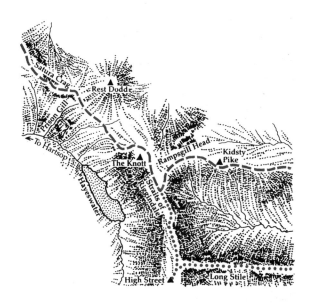

The path descends slightly, just above the fence, to cross Prison Gill. At this stream it passes the bottom end of a broken wall, then climbs gently. The fence below now decides to be a wall again, and here the path leaves it, and contours through boggy ground to pass through a broken wall. Go up a slight rise to an area of peat-hags and then a stony ascent to a cairned path junction. A wall runs across ahead: the steep path to Hartsop descends to the right. Turn left, up a stony path below the wall. The path bends round right, to reach the col at the back of Knott.

Those on whom the sun is shining can now make the attractive LONG STILE diversion over High Street. So as not to confuse further those around whom the mist is wrapped, consideration of this variant is deferred to the end of the section.

KNOTT: The wall has diverted to take in the summit of Knott, and now descends from the right to rejoin the path. Continue along the path, with the wall on the right, for 400m/yds and no more. As path and wall start to descend, a smaller path turns sharply back left. (If you find yourself between the wall and a steep drop on the left, you have overshot and reached Riggindale Straits.)

The path runs along the edge of the summit plateau of Rampsgill Head, always with steep drop to its right, and bends right to an eastward direction. It descends slightly then climbs to the summit of Kidsty Pike.

In 19th-century Lakeland, one of the springtime chores was climbing up to eagle nests and wrecking them. Eagles have now returned to Lakeland, and have been nesting for thirty years at the head of Mardale.

These are odd eagles. Aquila Chrysaetos requires 20 square miles of empty land, and 'empty' doesn't usually involve quite so many wandering humans as are found in the Lake District. Incidentally, spotting eagles is rather like falling in love: if you're not sure whether you have or not, then you haven't. Even from a distance, the eagle's slow wingbeats mean you instantly recognise that here is a bird twice as big as anything else in the sky.

KIDSTY PIKE: Go down the grassy ridge eastward on a gentle path. At Kidsty Howes the ground steepens, the ridge-crest turns slightly right and

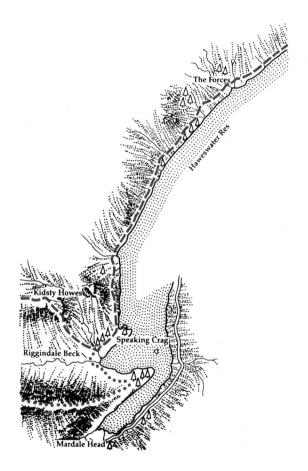

The Forces

Haweswater Res

Kidsty Howes

Speaking Crag

Riggindale Beck

Mardale Head

becomes a sharp spur. The path twists down between rocky outcrops, immediately left of the spur crest. This final part of the descent is uncomfortably steep for feet with nearly a week's walking behind them.

Open slopes lead out slightly right, then straight down to the reservoir side.

Formerly, Mardale had a character of its own, greener and more peaceful than the valleys of the west. The church with its square stone tower was smaller than the yew trees in its own graveyard; but from the fellside above, you could look down between the branches to its slate roof. Mardale was drowned in 1937, to provide water for the homes and factories of Manchester.

SPEAKING CRAG: Turn left across the stone footbridge of Randale Beck and along the bottom of a plantation. The promontory sticking into the lake on the right is Speaking Crag, where, before the rising of the waters, a fine echo could be obtained off the opposite wall of Mardale. The path along the lakeside is clear and well-built, if rough. It was made by Manchester Corporation in compensation for the flooding of the earlier road up the valley.

After 2½ miles (4 km) of lakeside, the path crosses a substantial concrete footbridge below the Forces (waterfalls) of Measand Beck. It now becomes a stony track. Various strange dangers are warned of by notices along the way: my favourites are

Drinking Water
DANGER!

and the one forbidding us to damage stones on the reservoir bed. Maybe I'm an innocent, it hadn't

occurred to me to damage stones on the reservoir bed.

The track descends through a gate into the plantation (the warning notice here is of 'Algal Scum'), and bends back right to run down onto a lower track. Turn left along this, to descend to a tarred lane.

BURNBANKS: Go straight across, onto a woodland footpath signposted 'Naddle Bridge'. It rejoins the road at that bridge. Cross the river by the old pack-horse bridge hidden behind the road one.

The path continues downstream, passing the fine Thornthwaite Force. The woodland here has at least six species. Linger and identify these – for in another mile, Lakeland will be merely a memory. Pass Park Bridge on the left, and continue on a faint track between river (left) and power line (right). Go through one gate (stile alongside) and up a short rise to a second.

Go through this gate, and continue up to right, next

to the fence. At a stile on the right, traverse off left to pass below the handsome restored barns of Highpark Buildings. The path here is not clear, but the next stile ahead can usually be seen.

Contour forward over three stiles, the last just above Rawhead Farm. Go down the farm's driveway to the road, and straight across to a footpath sign. This points down the boggy field towards Rosgill Bridge. At the field's bottom right corner, a ladder stile leads out onto the road. (Rosgill Bridge, 50m/yds ahead, is admired but not crossed by the Coast-to-Coast.)

ROSGILL BRIDGE: Turn right (gate and stile) onto a track (sign 'Coast-to-Coast'). Go through a green gate after 100m/yds, and follow the wall on the left. A slate sign 'footpath' points ahead through a gap in the wall. With the wall, and later a fence, on the left, go forward below the house called Goodcroft.

Once past it, look back at this house. Ignoring the new gable pointing towards you, you can see the original structure of the Lake District long house – a design brought by the Norsemen. The huge door was matched by another in the back wall; with both doors open to the wind, the space between could be used as threshing floor. The tiresome task of bashing apart the grain and the straw occupied much of the winter, but could at least be carried out under cover. (We still call the way into a house the 'threshold'.) The smaller part of the house, to left of the great door, would be for animals: the larger part for humans. The swayback line of the roof shows the great age of the timbers below the slates.

At the field's end the way crosses the handsome Parish Crag Bridge and turns straight uphill. At the top of the field, cross two ladder stiles through farm buildings to the corner of the tarred lane. Continue ahead, uphill, for 100m/yds. Turn left across a stile, then a ladder stile – this is the line of the right of way, and avoids the bog on the permissive path further up the hill.

Just beyond the ladder stile is the line of a field-edge earthwork. Head half-right across the field corner, passing under power lines, to the corner of a wall. Follow the wall round the top edge of the field and then descending to the left. A ladder-stile ahead leads into a field spotted with erratic boulders – most of these are of the Shap Granite, but one grey one shows pinkish where a corner has been knocked off, and is the last of the Lakeland rhyolite.

Turn right onto a small path that traverses, gradually leaving the wall. At the brow ahead, a small waymark post marks the point above a hidden ladder-stile. Descend to the track, and turn left over the Abbey Bridge.

Turn left too sharply, though, and you find yourself between narrowing walls above a sudden drop into the River Lowther. For here has been reconstructed an ancient sheep-dip. The 'diving board' was recovered from the riverbed; the rest has been rebuilt with fresh stone but ancient technique. The sheep leap into the river and swim across – it's a fine sight to see them fly out into the air with their legs stretched out like racehorses. The original dip was built by the 'worker priests' of the Premon-

stratensian Abbey immediately upstream. It was just one of the modern agricultural improvements they made on their way to becoming the most prosperous inhabitants of every valley they settled. (Not having wives and children to support may have helped, too.) Today's farmer reckons the simple riverwater dip makes the sheep nice and fluffy so they fetch a better price. But maybe he just likes to see them leap off the diving board with their legs out.

SHAP ABBEY: Turn left, away from the abbey. In the open field, leave the concrete track to go up the grass and rejoin it higher up.

The track leaves the field at a cattle-grid, but a stone gap-stile on the left lets you parallel its course behind the field-wall. The track meets the corner of the public road, and a footpath sign 'Keld Lane' points right, down a green lane. This is stony, between stone walls, and bordered with hawthorn and nettles (shorts-wearers may prefer the road).

At its end, follow the road left for 50m/yds. The road turns left, but another walled lane leads to the right. Follow this for just 20m/yds, then turn off left at a gap-stile.

Here are green fields enclosed by pale limestone walls. The edge of the green field, with a pale limestone wall on the left, leads past the massive Goggleby Stone. It's as good as its name, a lump of pink granite, overhanging on all sides, and not raised by man but dropped by glacier. At the field end two gap-stiles lead into a long narrow field. The gate at the foot of this opens into the back of Shap, with the main street just ahead.

VARIANT: LONG STILE (includes HIGH STREET)

This is scarcely longer than the main route, but it is more demanding; sure feet are required for the initial drop off the plateau.

KNOTT: The wall corner descends from the summit of Knott, to rejoin the stony path at the little col. Continue forward, with the wall on the right, descending into the narrow place that is Riggindale Straights. Here the path is squeezed between the wall and steep drops on the left.

The path goes through a wall gap; here is the ancient Roman road that ran along the top of High Street. Pass back through the wall, and follow it to the trig at the summit of High Street.

Turn back, and head slightly away right from wall and path for 200m/yds to a cairn at the edge of the summit plateau. Descend the ridge beyond, which is steep with some rock and some stony scree, to the col of Caspal Gate. After a slight rise, the sharp and interesting ridge continues – the path is mostly to the right of the crest, with views onto Blea Water.

VARIANT: ULLSWATER AND BAMPTON

With the wind down, and rain blowing horizontally across the ridge, Kidsty Pike can be no fun at all. Haweswater is a pretty good lake, considering it's a reservoir, but nothing can compare with Ullswater. So those who take this low-level option needn't feel short-changed, especially as they get a couple of extra miles for their money. (The necessary map, Outdoor Leisure 5, can be bought in Patterdale.)

PATTERDALE: From the western part of the village, beside the school, take the farm road to Side Farm. Go through this farm and turn left onto the wide, smooth path. (The upper path is just as nice, but less smooth.) The path leads round below the outcrop of Silver Crag. Below Birk Fell, wooded slopes drop steeply into the water. The views are good, especially back over the left shoulder to the mountains clustered round the head of the lake.

The path turns slightly inland, to pass above Scalehow Wood with a stone wall on its left. At Sandwick turn left down the tarred road for 100m/yds. The path continues through a succession of wooden gates through the oaks of Hallinhag Wood. Pass above Waternook, and look out for the gate and wooden steps down left to HOWTOWN pier.

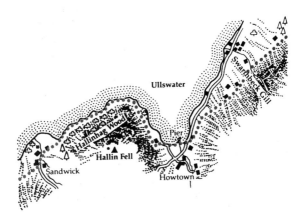

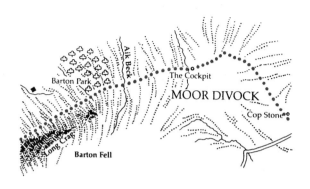

Walk past the pier to the road, and cross to a field gate with footpath sign. White-topped waymarks cross the field to steps to the right of a house. Go through a gate, to the track above.

The track leads left along the top of the enclosed land. It offers easy walking on a firm grassy surface. A small stone bridge crosses the Swarthbeck below its impressive gorge. At Auterstone the track slants uphill below the crags (sign 'Moor Divock'). Below Long Crag, a fine cairn stands above the track (GR461213). This is a place for a pause, for there is a fine final view back along Ullswater.

The track passes along the top edge of the trees of Barton Park, and dips in and out of the little lime-stone gorge of Aik Beck. Continue forward on the same level; the track is many-rutted and muddy, and not distinct from other wheelmarks across the moor. It becomes clear again as it rounds the curve of the slope to the ford of Elder Beck. Just beyond the beck is a fallen stone circle set in short green grass: this is the COCKPIT.

Continue in the same direction (north-east), across the stone circle, on a faint wet track, to meet a much clearer one at a signpost. Turn right (Helton). The track crosses the moor top, south-east. At an erratic boulder (the Cop Stone) on the left, branch off on a small side-path to cross a road. (The bridleway sign of the main track is 100m/yds to the right.) A bracken path leads to a ladder stile. Go down a long narrow field to the gate in its bottom left corner, and on a walled green way beyond.

After another gate, continue to the bottom of the field on the left, and then cross its bottom edge (thus not trampling the hay crop on the right of way). From this field's corner, four stiles lead north-east to the edge of HELTON.

Go towards the village for 50m/yds, then turn right between houses to cross the road beyond. A path between hedges leads down to the River Lowther, with a footbridge 100m/yds upstream. A green track beyond leads up to the road.

The field path by Whale is passable, and can be used to eliminate road-walking. Otherwise, turn right along the road for a mile (almost 2km) to a T-junction with phone box. Cross into the field, and head down half-left to a high suspension bridge over the river. On the far bank, a riverside path leads upstream to the road between the Bamptons. Turn left, over one bridge, and left again over

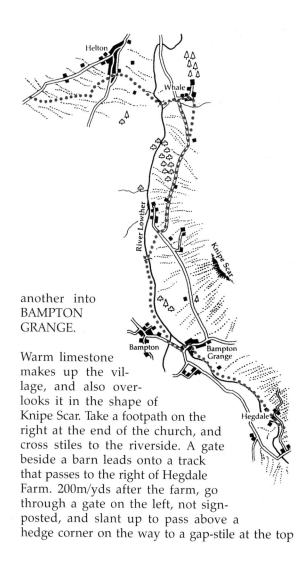

Helton

Whale

River Lowther

Knipe Scar

another into
BAMPTON
GRANGE.

Bampton

Bampton
Grange

Warm limestone
makes up the vil-
lage, and also over-
looks it in the shape of
Knipe Scar. Take a footpath on the
right at the end of the church, and
cross stiles to the riverside. A gate
beside a barn leads onto a track
that passes to the right of Hegdale
Farm. 200m/yds after the farm, go
through a gate on the left, not signposted, and slant up to pass above a
hedge corner on the way to a gap-stile at the top

Hegdale

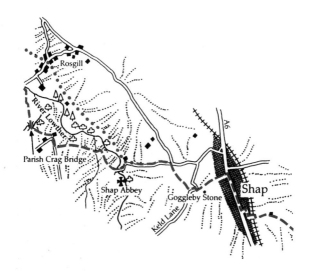

right corner of the field. Another stile leads into Rosgill.

Cross the road to a gap-stile between houses just up left. The way contours forward, through gap-stiles, to the top edge of a wood. A track leads to abandoned sheds, which are bypassed on the left following waymarks. Beyond, take the stile slightly up left, not the gate ahead.

The right of way follows the bottom edges of fields, just above the steeper drop to the Lowther's floodplain. It is supplied with ladder stiles. The last of these, just above a house, leads onto the concrete track just above Shap Abbey.

Section 6:

The Limestone Plateau

As the years go by, some things get better and others get worse. What are better are the field paths – where early explorers tore their breeches on the barbed wire, we now find waymarks and tidy stiles. What's lost, though, is limestone pavement. This part of the route once ran high over ground of clints and grikes (just like in secondary school geography). Wainwright's first edition gave instruction in the art of climbing drystone walls.

What's left is limestone grassland. Limestone grassland is smooth and short. Limestone grassland is fast. In no time at all the brief ugly bit – the railway, and the motorway, and the Shap cement works – has dropped below the rounded green horizon. On Crosby Ravensworth Moor there's a bit (a very small bit) of limestone pavement, and limestone rocks like rotten teeth stick out of the sides of the dry valley. And another gain is Orton: a small, grey village with flowers and a river running through.

Broad green tracks lead onward, dipping to the green hollow of Smardale – even the roadbed of the little bridge is green, as is the river water underneath. Intricate fieldwork leads to Kirkby Stephen. Here's a friendly little market town, a place to relax if you've taken the limestone hard and fast in a single day.

DIFFICULTIES: Indistinct path over Crosby Ravensworth Fell – difficult in mist. Tiresome two-mile (3km) roadwalk past Mazon Wath. Field edge navigation from Smardale Fell onwards.

SHAP to KIRKBY STEPHEN, 19 miles (30km): 2,000ft (600m). GOING: easy.

Leave the main street opposite the King's Arms, entering Moss Grove (sign: 'Hardendale'). In 100m/yds a Coast-to-Coast sign indicates the right turn to the railway bridge. ('Max laden weight 3 tonnes' – but the rucksack isn't that bad, really!) After the bridge the track turns right and in 50m/yds left. It is now stony, between stone walls, and climbs for 300m/yds to a junction. The right fork leads after 50m/yds into a field.

A footbridge over the motorway is visible directly ahead, across two fields. Go straight to it, over two gap-stiles.

Though we are now on limestone, the fields following the motorway are speckled with boulders of granite. These originate at an outcrop a few miles south of the route. Because of its large pink crystals, this 'Shap Pink Granite' is easily recognisable wherever the glaciers have carried it. Some of these boulders are going the same way as ourselves, and have been seen, as we shall be, crossing the Vale of York. (They will have got there by a longer route, circling north by way of the A66 through the Stainmore Gap.) Others travelled as far south as Shropshire.

Cross the M6 MOTORWAY and turn right along the top of the embankment for 300m/yds. Where a broken wall crosses, a faint path heads up left, starting just below a wall corner and crossing two stiles at the brow of the hill to a gate beyond. The road ahead is crossed at footpath signposts (Hardendale).

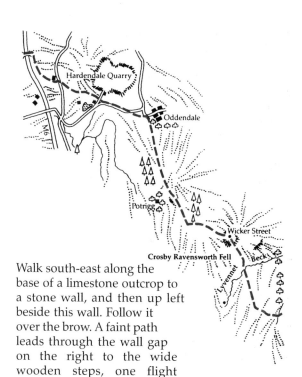

Walk south-east along the
base of a limestone outcrop to
a stone wall, and then up left
beside this wall. Follow it
over the brow. A faint path
leads through the wall gap
on the right to the wide
wooden steps, one flight
down and one flight up, at the entrance to the huge
Hardendale Quarry. The hill you've just come
around, Hardendale Nab, ends abruptly, its eastern
half having been carried away and made into
cement.

The steps lead up onto a wide gravel track heading
east. When this bends left, an unmarked right of
way runs forward to a field corner, then half-left to
the gap in the shelter-belt where the lane enters
ODDENDALE.

Turn right at this lane bend, with the shelter-trees to the left, onto a stony track. This heads up over grassland, passing to the right of a skyline cairn. It goes left of a large plantation and reaches the scattered trees around Potrigg. Do not enter the large enclosure, but keep to left of its stone wall on a very faint green track. From here, note the plantation in the valley bottom, and the two trees on the horizon beyond. The permissive path runs round the right-hand end of the plantation, and to the right of the two trees.

400m/yds after leaving the Potrigg wall corner, watch out for a waymark alongside the track, with sign alongside (GR598118). The following section is marked with these waymarks, at rather wide intervals. They are carved 'C>C': note that the central chevron of this message is not a direction-of-travel arrow!

Turn off here (some 200m/yds north of the line marked on the OS strip-map) to descend to the south corner of the plantation. Further waymarks lead straight up the slope opposite, to the metal 'Ancient Monument' sign at the summit of Wicker Street. (Wicker Street is a Roman road, just visible on the ground, crossed near the top of the slope.)

WICKER STREET: Here is a place to pause; the two trees noted earlier are growing out of a fine piece of limestone pavement. This is a sample of the ground ahead: ground which, for want of legal access, we shall walk below on roads.

A small path leads south-east (116 degrees), past a

low wall circle and across an area of bare limestone. Where a green bridleway track crosses, a stone circle is 100m/yds off-route on the left. It's built entirely of Shap erratics, all now fallen. The next waymark stands beside a still finer erratic, a very noticeable stone. The way, faintly marked, descends across Lyvennet Beck, and continues uphill on what looks like a scruffy track (but is actually natural erosion). Where this ends, slant up to join the stone wall on the left.

A green path through heather runs alongside the wall. The way is crossed by a sharp stream valley, and then by a dry valley where a bridleway sign points right 'Orton'. 100m/yds up this valley lies the rough pile of stones that is 'Robin Hood's Grave', which is, of course, a reminder of our (by now not quite so distant) end-point. It's odd to find a tumulus placed in such a hidden hollow. However, the books do say 'the location of Robin Hood's Grave is unknown' – this, clearly, is that unknown place.

ROBIN HOOD'S GRAVE: Continue up the dry valley. At once it divides, and the right fork leads south below the heather. Gradually getting shallower, the valley leads to a stile over the stone wall at the brow of the moor.

Go down the right-hand edge of the field to two empty gateways, but go through neither of these, passing left, to a marked stile. Orton is now visible ahead. Go down with a wall on the left, over a series of stiles marked with white paint, aiming just to right of the church. A final stile leads into the graveyard. Turn right at the corner of the church to

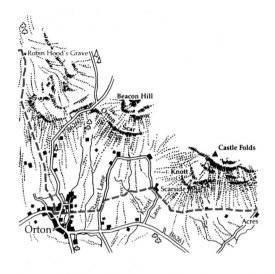

the stocks. The village post office shop is 50m/yds away on the right (GR621083, not where it's marked on OS map).

ORTON: Go down the southward (Tebay) road, and turn left through the car park at the village hall to a signed footpath by the bus shelter. It crosses playing fields, a white footbridge and a street to become a narrow path between gardens, then follows a long narrow field to reach Street Lane.

100m/yds up left, a bridleway sign points right across a stile. Follow the field edge past a clump of trees into a wide green way between walls. Scarside Farm (not Scar Side two words Farm) is visible ahead, and after the next field a muddy tractor track leads there through gates.

Turn right along the tarred lane past the farm to a gate and stile on the left. Cross the field, with a fence on your left, to the Knott Lane track. Immediately opposite is the sign 'Coast-to-Coast'.

The bridleway contours east through a succession of gap-stiles, passing below a fine barn after the fourth of them. Now come three gap-stiles in quick succession. The faint path contours across a wide field, above another barn, to reach a gate and gap-stile under a sycamore clump. Cross the final field to the double gate onto the road at Acres Farm.

Turn left along the road. It leads up to Sunbiggin Farm, where it bends right. At Stony Head it becomes a rough track.

After 800m/yds this bends left, but a wide green way leads ahead. At the top of the slope bear slightly right onto a narrowing green track through

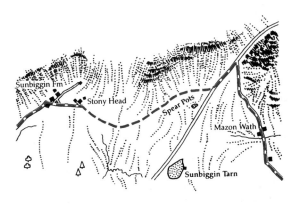

the heather (bearing 77 degrees) to a gap-stile. Beyond the wall, the ground is rough grass with a little path that is marked with yellow-topped poles. Just above the path is a small pothole: a deep grass dip with a rocky cave in the bottom. The mysterious hole leads down to an abandoned fertiliser sack. At the bottom of the slope is the pool of Spear Pots, a noisy nest-site for gulls in late spring.

After 400m/yds bear right on a green track to join the road. This leads up to a junction, where it is necessary to double back right on the side-road (sign-posted Newbiggin). This leads down past Mazon Wath, where it crosses a cattle grid. It then rises gradually for another mile (1.5 km) to cross another cattle grid.

Just past the grid a faint green track turns off left. After 300m/yds this moves away from the accompanying wall: the reason is the small swamp of Ewefell Mire. A clearer track leads back left to a gate. It continues as a green sunken way past a barn on the right. Now keep alongside the wall on the right, not taking less-marked tracks rising to left. The correct track dips in and out of a dry valley to reach the large hoarding advertising the facilities of nearby Bents Farm.

The green track continues beside the wall for 400m/yds, to end at a gate. Continue along the same wall, soon crossing by a way marked stile to its right-hand side. The wall, and a faint path, cross the crest of Begin Hill, to descend through small outcrops. At the bottom corner stands a railway cottage, its walls partly clad in slates. Go down into

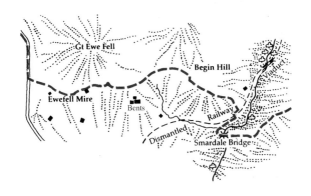

this corner (to avoid damaging the archaeology), then right, to the bridge over the abandoned railway. The archaeology on Begin Hill, a Bronze Age settlement, is invisible to untutored eyes.

Across the bridge turn right, alongside the railway. After 200m/yds, drop off left to the bridge which is visible below.

SMARDALE BRIDGE: From the bridge a stony track climbs steeply, then turns left to become grassy and slant uphill above a stone wall. After a gentle mile (1.5 km) of ascent, the wall bends away slightly left at a four-way signpost. Here the way continues in the same north-easterly direction, slanting uphill to find another stone wall around the curve of the slope. You look across the fertile flatland of the Vale of Eden to flat-topped Mallerstang on the right, and Nine Standards Rigg ahead.

After today's fast flatness, tomorrow consists simply of the long crossing of this single hill. Turn slightly right (east) to follow the wall down the slope of Limekiln Hill. There is no clear path: keep 50m/yds out to the right of the wall to discover the limekiln itself. Its stone arch is half-buried in the hill. Rejoin the wall, to a ladder stile onto the road below.

Follow the road right for 150m/yds, then sharp left (sign 'Waitby'). After another 150m/yds, a high gap-stile and Coast-to-Coast sign lead into a field on the right. The bridge under the Settle-Carlisle railway can be seen ahead. Cross two fields and pass to the right of a field barn to reach it.

Walk half-right out into the field beyond, passing stony humps of an ancient settlement to find a waymarked gap-stile in the field's back right corner. Head downhill into a little dry valley, then ease up right to a marked gap-stile in the facing wall.

Go down the right-hand side of the field to a gate. A track leads between the piers of a former railway bridge into Greenriggs Farm. The track bends right then left between the buildings, and becomes a patchily-tarred lane. In 800m/yds it reaches the beginning of Kirkby Stephen. Ignore the first turn-off to right, leading to a phone box. Any subsequent turning on the right leads to the town's main street.

NOTE TO SECTION 6: It is possible to include the limestone pavement, by way of a bridleway through the Nature Reserve. This gives a more interesting walk: however it means a totally new

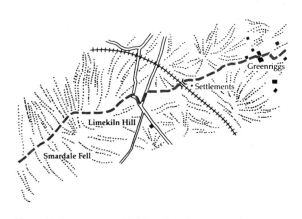

line all the way to Kirkby Stephen – perhaps too gross a deviation from the traditional Coast-to-Coast.

From Orton take the field bridleway to Scar Side, and the footpath (marked as a bridleway) through the limestone to Asby Winderwath Common. Bridleway and footpath, all well-waymarked, lead east by Asby Grange to Little Asby, and then dip into the charming Potts Valley to reach Crosby Garrett by a descending green lane with fine views.

The eastward footpath out of the village is blocked by nettle and burdock, but roads lead to a bridge over a disused railway a mile (1.5km) west of Kirkby Stephen. A footpath by Bloody Bones Lane leads into the town.

Section 7

Nine Standards Rigg

A lot of English hills are like Nine Standards: flat-topped, not particularly steep-sided, and made of peat with odd bits of gravel. Much of the Pennine Way is on such ground, and people enjoy the Pennine Way. So let's just say that Nine Standards is the Coast-to-Coast's brief tribute to the other long walk. If you really enjoy Nine Standards, then maybe you're on the wrong path ...

Then again, on a spring morning with the skylarks up, Nine Standards does have a magic of its own. Bog cotton nods in the breeze, and beyond the bog cotton you're looking at half of northern England and even a corner of Scotland. And the Nine Standards, of which there are ten, are a fine waymark at the watershed of England. Walkers don't like peat: and peat doesn't like walkers. Two routes off Nine Standards are presented, for different parts of the year, as seasonal permissive paths. Each way down is long and boggy, and the deep, slithery holes of the summit plateau are common to both. From December to April, though, you'll be diverted onto a bridleway route that doesn't get to the top at all.

DIFFICULTIES: Slippery peat on Nine Standards is followed by slippery limestone mud – heavy going in the wet. Two of the seasonal routes are off the edge of the OS strip-map: only the August to November path is covered. The winter (December to April) route is tricky in mist at Dukerdale Head.

KIRKBY STEPHEN TO KELD, 11 miles (18km): 2,000ft (600m). GOING: hard.

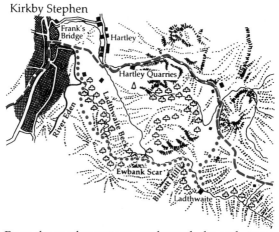

From the market square, go through the arch oppo-site the Pennine Hotel to a narrow footway. At the street beyond, steps lead down to the handsome packhorse bridge, Frank's Bridge.

The road that follows is particularly unattractive as it passes Hartley Quarry. Here is an alternative route that is very much prettier, but also rather harder.

LADTHWAITE VARIANT:

Turn right onto the dog-walking path, and where the tarred path leads on towards Hartley, turn off right along the grassy river-bank. A fine barn here is built of bockram, which is either a very sandy limestone or a very limey sandstone. Later in the

83

walk, at Richmond, this building material is referred to as 'bastard'.

Beyond the bastard barn, a footbridge hidden in deep foliage leads onto a woodland path – the deeply sunken track of the original bridleway is alongside. At the end of the wood, turn up left through a field gate: there is no signpost, and the footpath from here is invisible on the ground. Head up the field to rejoin its left-hand wall, which leads round to the bridge over the former railway and then up into a green lane.

The lane ends above the deep, wooded valley of Ladthwaite Beck. Go down through a field gate to the left of a barn. A wall on the left leads down into the wood. Now various poorly-defined paths traverse upstream through the wood. If low branches and loose earth are too annoying, a way can be made along the wood's top edge, but this would miss the fine crag that forms the opposite wall of the valley.

A scruffy fence descending through the wood has a gate at its top end, just above the trees. Go up the sharp slope above, to the right of trees, with a glimpse of Nine Standards looking from here like a rather high hill. Contour left to join the stream, which runs round the base of the steep, rocky spur of Birkett Hill.

A wall stile leads into a flat, muddy field and to a stile before Ladthwaite Farm (do not shortcut left across the stream, as a high wall stands in the way of the exit track). The farm's entrance track crosses the beck and after 400m/yds bends left towards a stone hut, with spoil heaps above right. The right of way mounts the steep grass on the right, then traverses above the spoil heap, following old fence posts and a line of sink holes. It rejoins the track to cross the cattle grid to the top of the Hartley road.

EASIER WAY (HARTLEY QUARRY)

For the easier way, after crossing Frank's Bridge, again take the dog-walking path to right along the riverbank. After a kissing gate the path, now tarred, runs uphill. Before a second kissing gate, a footpath sign points half-right, to a stone gap built into a fence. Follow the left-hand side of the field round to a lane.

Turn left down the lane to a footbridge on the right. Here a homemade sign indicates 'Hikers and Walkers: Nine Standards and Whitby'. (For Whitby, follow the Coast-to-Coast for 105 miles/170km, then turn left at the North Sea.) The road to the right bends uphill, but a path continues ahead to the right of a garage, and rejoins the road above.

Turn right, uphill. For the first few steps the road is busy with quarry traffic, but then bends left at the piers of a demolished railway bridge (the same demolished railway that we passed over at Smardale). For the next half-mile, roadside hedges are white with lung-damaging dust from the quarry, but the view soon improves to the wooded back of Hartley Hill, backed by the limestone lumps of Mallerstang and Wild Boar Fell. The road crosses the bed of the Hartley Beck, then ends at a gate.

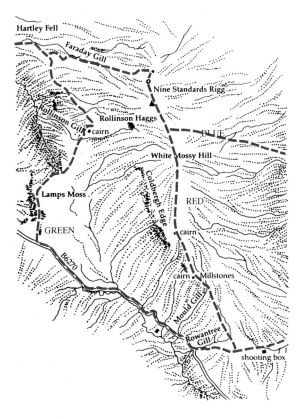

HARTLEY ROAD TOP: The rough track ahead (sign: 'Rollinson Haggs') rises to another gate, then right to join a stone wall and follow it uphill. At the 450m contour, wall and track bend right, and after another 250m/yds is the signboard announcing the start of the diverging routes.

RED ROUTE (May-July): BLUE ROUTE (August-November) to Nine Standards Rigg

HARTLEY FELL: Turn left on a grassy track, which slants left then goes uphill to right of Faraday Gill. Above the stream's rocky section, a narrow railed footbridge crosses it – this may be impossible for the very bulky rucksack-carrier. The path continues uphill for a soggy 500m/yds, then contours left (north-east) before the final slope to the ten tall cairns that are the Nine Standards.

Turn south, to the viewpoint cairn (it looks like a trig point) and then another 300m/yds rather east of south to something else that looks like a trig point but, this time, is one. Continue (155 degrees) to a sign, after which the path into the col is clear as it plunges into the heart of monstrous peat hags. Wallow through the hags, to reach the signpost where RED and BLUE descent routes diverge.

RED ROUTE: by Coldbergh Edge

The path down Coldbergh Edge is gentle and pleasant, but has a slight tendency to get lost in mist. If this does happen, only a compass will get you down this feature-less slope to roughly the right place.

The path crosses the low lump of White Mossy Hill slightly east of south, then turns south and descends to the left of the ill-defined crest to a shelter cairn (marked 'pile of stones') on Coldbergh Edge. Here it bends slightly left, to a tall narrow cairn (marked 'stone') at Millstones. This tapered column appears to have been built of bits of millstone that broke before they were finished.

The view ahead into Yorkshire is dispiriting. Nothing is seen but flat moorland and low, obviously boggy hills. Things are better than they seem: hidden in the hollows are deep, green valleys, limestone crags, and biscuit-coloured villages selling ice cream and picture postcards.

The path edges round the head of Mould Gill to reach a rough, bulldozed track. Follow this, left, to a black iron hut. A footbridge is just below. The peaty path continues downhill to the left of the stream, passing above smart new grouse-butts. A fence arrives from the left. The path continues between fence and stream for 800m/yds to the signboard where the Blue Route rejoins.

The upland peats of the Pennines spread over almost a hundred miles: you could walk from Haltwhistle to Skipton and never have dry feet. In geological terms, peat is a ground-covering almost as temporary as snow. It formed in an eyeblink of time, the brief 2,000 years after the ice age when it was warm enough for plants to grow, but not warm enough for them to rot. Simple chemical breakdown, unassisted by bacteria, quickly made the spongy mass so acid that when the bacteria did arrive, they could not stomach it.

Only the tough grass topping holds the peat in place. Once this is broken, by small streams, by sheep, or by the feet of walkers, the peat washes out from under, to form the black-sided slimy hollows that people of the Pennines call 'groughs'. Once formed, groughs must grow, and another 10,000 years should see the end of bog problems on Nine Standards.

BLUE ROUTE: by Whitsundale Beck

From the signpost at Rollinson Haggs, the left-hand path heads just south of east (bearing 100 degrees). It's a wide muddy streak, marked by poles which, at 60m/yds apart, are not necessarily intervisible in mist. The path descends to a Coast-to-Coast sign above the Whitsundale Beck. Here it turns right, to contour peaty slopes above the stream for 1½ miles (2km).

After a stile at Fawcett Gate, a wall crosses ahead, and there the path turns right, away from the stream, at a Coast-to-Coast sign. It goes over the boggy base of the spur to a signboard beside Ney Gill. Here the various routes rejoin.

GREEN ROUTE (December-April) by Lamps Moss

History, not reason, dictates our bridleways. The path is formed of two sled-gangs: convenient if you want to bring down minerals from Rollinson Haggs, but if you just want to get to Keld, you may resent the unnecessary 60m (200ft) climb to the fingerpost.

However, the ground is steeper and more interesting than the flat summit, and the view into the end of Dukerdale is quite spectacular. Even the B6270 is a road that would rather like to be a real footpath, as it clings to the side of its empty valley and dips in and out of streams.

HARTLEY FELL: Stay on the track alongside the

stone wall. After 400m/yds it slants away from the wall between two swallow holes. At the top of this rise it enters a morass – fork slightly right, cross a stream, and head uphill to rejoin the track below the eroded hole of the disused quarry. Little more than a grass path, the way slants up through rushes to a fingerpost (Coast-to-Coast) at the 580m contour.

Turn right, downhill, to a small ruin – this will be the point of reference when the fingerpost has fallen down and rotted. The small path zigzags down, to right of the Rollinson Gill stream, then turns left to cross it and contours to meet a stone wall.

Follow the wall around the cliffed head of Dukerdale. At its corner, head just south of west (255 degrees), to the right of peaty heather, up a pathless slope of grass and bare limestone. Marvel at the fact that here, for the first time since St Bees, the word 'west' has appeared in the route description, and watch carefully for a green track at the top of the slope. This runs south, to reach the moor road.

Turn left, for nearly 2 miles (3km). Just after the culvert of the Rowantree Gill, a fingerpost points left to indicate the right of way, which soon meets a rough, bulldozed track. The lack of a path suggests that many continue 100m/yds to take the track from its bottom end (marked 'Private Road').

Turn left along the track, which leads over the moor to a black iron hut. A footbridge is just below. The peaty path continues downhill to the left of the

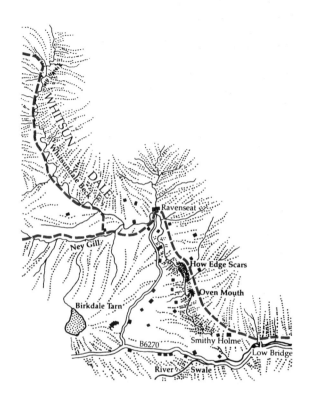

stream, passing above smart, new grouse-butts. A fence arrives from the left. The path continues between fence and stream for 800m/yds to the sign-board where the Blue Route rejoins.

NEY GILL SIGNPOST: The three seasonal routes have now rejoined. Do not cross the Ney Gill yet:

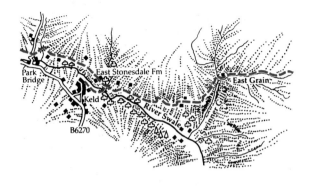

first go downstream for 100m/yds to a sign (Keld) pointing right. Follow the wall on the left to a gated gap. A smaller path leads down to the stream side, which is followed to Ravenseat Bridge.

RAVENSEAT: After the first, stone bridge comes a second, wooden one. The path, through a gate on the right, is small and slippery: there's limestone in this mud. It heads downstream, slightly above the beck, through gap stiles. Yellow paint splashes are on gateposts and barn ends.

The path runs along the top of the wooded gorge of How Edge Scars: there's a fine view down to the water at the start, also at the far end, Oven Mouth. From here the way contours forward, to pass along the bottom of a stone enclosure. The hill path drops gradually past a signpost to the farm buildings at

Smithy Holme.

The stones-and-mud access track slants down to the left. Just before the final drop to Low Bridge, a footpath (with waymark post) forks off left. This runs along the top of Cotterby Scar, above the river, then continues on the same level to meet the hill road above Park Bridge.

A gated track continues directly opposite (East Stonesdale Farm). It runs above the river, with views to the rooftops of Keld on the other side. At East Stonesdale farmyard, a track arriving from above is the route of the Pennine Way. The two long paths descend together to the East Gill, which has a neat little waterfall at this point. Ahead is the great gorge of upper Swale: but our route will climb up left into an equally spectacular side-valley. First, though, a path down right leads to a footbridge and a climbing cobbled path into the village of Keld.

Section 8:
Swaledale

Swaledale reaches east, from here in the heart of the Pennines all the way to the Vale of York. It's a valley of green fields, and grey-stone walls, with a tall grey-stone barn standing in every field. Along the rim lie long outcrops of grey limestone and grey-brown sandstone, and along the bottom runs the River Swale, bright on its bed of pebbles and breaking occasionally into gorge and waterfall.

You might well think that this long green valley would be the best way out of the Pennines – better, certainly, than the black-and-orange moorlands above, moorlands lacerated and scarred by a former mining industry. You might think that – but you'd be wrong.

In Gunnerside Gill you descend into landscape not just altered by man's activity but deliberately wrecked – here is erosion to give nightmares to the Lakeland footpath teams. Streams have been dammed then released to wash away hillsides and reveal the minerals below. In the bottom, beside the ruins of a smelting mill, a single stone crosses the river, laid as pavement for miners and their machinery. In a walk embracing sea-cliff and heather moor, high passes, lakesides and the bouncy hills of Cleveland, this stream bottom is one of the top moments.

The way rises across a lunar landscape of mine tailings, then drops – we couldn't ignore it – into green Swaledale. You pass along field tops, down to the riverbank where willows grow, and through shadowy woods with wild flowers and ancient yews. Reeth is made of the same green grass and grey stone as its surrounding fields.

In high summer, even gentle Swaledale can seem a busy place. An alternative route from Reeth is high, wild, very quiet, and crosses MARRICK MOOR to the green hollow of the MARSKE BECK.

And so, at nightfall, to the tall town of Richmond.

DIFFICULTIES: The drop into Gunnerside Gill is sudden and steep; the climb out again is steep, rocky, and with no clear path. After Surrender Bridge you enter the confusing network of Swaledale field paths. The ways are not well marked, and progress depends on spotting stiles and waymarks from one stone wall to the next.

KELD to RICHMOND, 20½ miles (33km): 2,800ft (850m). GOING: moderate/rough. MARRICK MOOR, MARSKE BECK variant adds 1½miles (2km): 500ft (150m)

Return to the footbridge, take a long, longing look down the Swale Gorge (the way by Gunnerside is even better, honest!) and turn right at the track above to cross East Gill. The track climbs up the side of the deep-cut valley, looking across to the wooded crag of Kisdon and the Pennine Way. After a zigzag, take the upper track to the derelict Crackpot Hall.

The track passes above the Hall and below a barn, then turns the sharp spur into Swinner Gill at a gate. Here it becomes a path traversing the steep slope to the mine buildings nestling in the hollow where the gill divides. The path crosses Hind Hill Beck to follow East Gill; it is rough and rocky as it

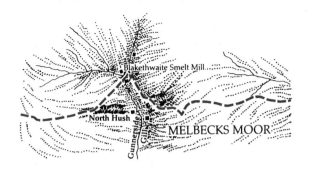

ascends to left of the stream. As the slope eases onto the moor plateau, the path becomes muddy, and meets a stony track running in from the right. Go straight across, onto a path that runs parallel with the track and rejoins it after 400m/yds.

The track runs east and easily over the moor top. As it starts to descend, it reaches an area of devastated stony ground, the beginning of the North Hush. Just past a stone-and-corrugated sheep shelter, a small cairned path branches off left. This goes down to the left of the artificial ravine, then slants down left, becoming eroded as the ground steepens. Here pause, to examine the route up the opposite face of the Gill.

Having descended most of the slope, the path turns back right; then left, on a green track, to the handsome one-slab footbridge beside the ruined Blakethwaite Smelt Mill.

GUNNERSIDE GILL: A path zigzags up the east side of the valley to a green track above. Turn right, down-valley. The track climbs gently below screes, then descends slightly, becoming a rough narrow path that's barely more than a sheep-trod.

After another 100m/yds the path starts to descend more steeply towards ruined buildings, and here, opposite the foot of North Hush, turn uphill. A much smaller path climbs the slope of grass and scree for 150 feet (50m vertical), i.e., for two or three minutes, then traverses right, into the ravine of Bunton Hush.

Here the upward gully divides. Go up inside the right-hand branch, for about five minutes, until it becomes shallow and grassy. Go up right, to a cairn, and up the spur that is the gully's right-hand (south) wall to another cairn just above.

Here we join a little-used track that comes up from stone enclosures on the right. It zigzags away to right and then back left. As the slope eases, the track runs forward across stony devastation to join a much wider and well-maintained shooters' track above.

This clear track runs eastward across the top of the moor through orange spoil-heaps. It passes an abandoned stone-crusher machine now serving as a fine wayside sculpture, then dips into a stony little ravine, that, if it were in Arizona, would certainly be referred to as a gulch. After crossing Level House Bridge, the track joins another, and runs down Old Gang Beck for two trouble-free miles (3

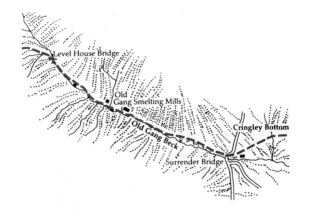

quick km) to the tarred road at Surrender Bridge. On the way it passes the lovingly-restored ruins of the Old Gang Smelting Mills.

Vaporised lead seeped up into Swaledale at the time of the Variscan Uplift (Africa Crunch) that raised the Pennines; it's been being taken out since the Romans. The track off Melbecks Moor was first formed by wooden sledges, bringing ore from the Old Gang Mines to the Old Gang Smelting Mills and the one below, at Surrender Bridge.

SURRENDER BRIDGE: Cross the road to a foot-path sign. Here are various paths and tracks: take the green track slightly left. It climbs gently above another ruined smelt mill, then bears left (70 degrees) across the moor to the ravine of Cringley Bottom. Green fields are across the ravine: the way forward will be along their top edge.

Descend steeply to cross the stream (no footbridge), and climb the further side to a stile. Follow the field-top wall. Where this drops away right, a stony track continues across the moor, then drops gently to Thirns Farm.

A concrete track climbs to Moorcock House, to become a stony field-top track. After nearly a mile (1.5 km) this drops towards the busy farm of Riddings, but here contour on a path above the farm, to rejoin the field-top wall for just 20m/yds. A gate leads into the top of the walled path that is Skelgate Lane. This leads down between blackthorn and dog rose. Where it turns left, a gate leads down towards the school. Slant left to a wall gap, but before the second wall gap take a stile below, to cross the end of the tiny football pitch to a walled path beside the school. The road below leads down

into REETH.

The centre of Reeth's market green is the centre of Swaledale. Over the rooftops of various useful facilities such as post office, information centre and a selection of ancient inns, you see the fields rising to a scarp of grey limestone, and dark heather moor-edge.

VARIANT: MARRICK MOOR, MARSKE BECK

Leave the market square by its top right (north-east) corner. Where the lane bends right, a footpath leads out into fields. Slant down to the river, to cross on the remains of a fallen footbridge. (If the water is high, leave Reeth rather by the regular route to cross Reeth Bridge: a footpath leads left up the east bank.)

Turn half-left to a gap-stile, and follow white paint marks up past a large barn. Slant right, up the field beyond, to a gated gap just above White House. Go straight up to a stony track, which climbs steeply to the rim of the moor at Fremington Edge.

Turn right, through a gate, and take a green track that slants half-left away from the Edge and over the moor top. As it fades out, go down to Owlands Farm directly below. Pass through the farm, and go straight up the field above (north) to a gap-stile. A very small path leads on north through the heather, passing to left of a wall corner, and descending to a stile above Ings Head.

Cross the road, and go straight down through gates

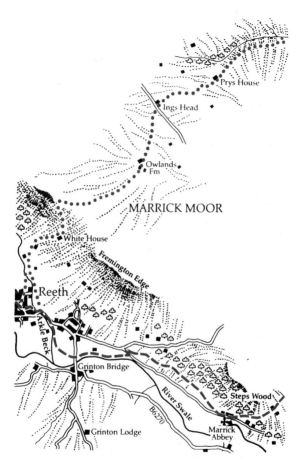

to the rough access track of Prys House. Turn right on this, but keep to the official bridleway, which leaves the track, follows the fence on the right, and rejoins the track after passing knolly remnants of old mine pits. Pass through Prys House to a way-marked gate, slant left to the wall on the left, and follow this to a gate at the top of a green track that slants down into the valley of the Marske Beck. This gentle hollow, with its generous lumps of bushy woodland, is a nice complement to the austere moorland above.

Turn right, along the stream's right bank, rising after a waymarked gate to pass above Telfit Farm onto its access track. Follow this for 100m/yds. Just after a stone barn, a waymarked gate on the left leads down towards the river: cross a stile on the left to find the handsome stone footbridge.

Slant right, up the field, to a wall corner, and head along above the wall to stone barns. Here begins a faint traversing track. Once across the tarred access track to Orgate Farm, a clearer track leads on, past the grand house at Clints, to Marske.

MAIN ROUTE: from REETH

The lane to right of the Post Office becomes tarred as it passes the Folk Museum. A few yards before its foot, turn left on a path that goes down to the bank of Arkle Beck. The beckside path leads down-stream, to pass under the road bridge and gain the roadside unexpectedly from beyond.

Now on top of Reeth Bridge, cross Arkle Beck and follow the road for 150m/yds to a footpath sign on the right (Grinton). The footpath passes to the right of buildings, then eases away from the river to a kissing gate. Head across a field to Grinton Bridge.

Cross the road (but not the bridge!) to the riverside footpath beyond. After 800m/yds, a stile leads onto the tarred access lane for Marrick Abbey. Turn right; or, to avoid tarmac, turn back left for 60m/yds to a stile. Turn back right, above a copse, and rise gently to a stile above a fence corner. The field path runs one field up from the road, then through gates directly towards the Abbey tower. Just past the Abbey, a gate leads left, to reach the flagstoned path that slants up through Steps Wood.

The 800-year-old stones are deeply worn; can we say that the anti-erosion measure is itself eroded? When in another 40 miles (60km) we reach the Cleveland Hills, it will be good to think that their stone slabs will, by the year 2,800 at the latest, be as well blended in as this. The path was built originally by monks, going up to the village to use the phone box, buy their Lottery tickets and claim their child benefit. (Hmm – at this point, serious consideration of history has been distracted by the ancient yew trees and fresh primroses of this delightful wood.)

A gate at the top of the wood leads to a field-bottom path and the stony track that becomes the lane into MARRICK village. Now follows the trickiest stile-finding of the entire walk.

Turn right at the phone box, and at the following road junction right again at a Coast-to-Coast sign. The road curves round to the foot of an uphill track. Turn up this (another Coast-to-Coast sign), and at its end, go ahead over three gap-stiles through tiny fields. Beyond is a triangle of mud with abandoned railway trucks, one of which is waymarked with yellow paint.

Cross the mud to a gate with a stile alongside. Go up to the left of sheds and up the left edge of a field to a gap-stile through a hedge. Turn half-right, to cross three marked stiles over the brow of the hill and descend a bank to the track near Nun Cote Nook.

Turn right along this track for 30m/yds through a gate to a triple signpost. Go straight down the field below, past a waymarked power-pole, to a gate just right of a barn. Head diagonally right down the field below, to a waymarked stile near its bottom corner. Two more marked stiles lead to Ellers. This house has no access track but a very pretty garden; the inhabitants can pluck hollyhocks from their upstairs windows. Go round it to a footbridge.

ELLERS: Do many abandon the Coast-to-Coast between Nine Standards and here? For the way, so eroded there, is here invisible. Cross the field diagonally right, to the gate in its top-right corner. Cross the field above on the same line, to the gate at its top right. A track runs across right, towards Hollins Farm. After 70m/yds, turn uphill, following yellow paint-splashes round to left of trees to a stile. Go up the long field beyond to its top right corner. After 50m/yds between fence and wall, a sign points right over the brow of the hill. Follow it to the signposted stile onto the road at Hardstiles Top. Well-named is this house: but the really hard stiles are now accomplished.

The road leads down right, to Marske Bridge; but again tarmac can be avoided by turning left for 150m/yds to a gate. Turn back right, and slant out

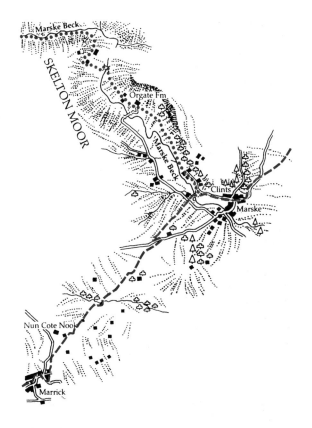

across the field to pass the left-hand corner of a plantation of oaks. Go straight down the field beyond, parallel to its left-hand fence, to a stile in a former gateway. Cross the road to a narrow, rotting gate, and a two-arch footbridge (Pillimire Bridge).

Slant up right, to the track above, and follow it to

the right, into MARSKE. Bear right to the phone box, and turn uphill onto the principal road through the village.

As the road descends after 500m/yds, a footpath sign points through a hedge gap on the right. The next hedge gap is north-east across a wide field. Cross two stiles, then bend slightly left (40 degrees) to find a third. Below is the footbridge, hidden under trees, across the Clapgate Beck.

Slant right up the slope beyond, past the top corner of a fenced enclosure, to the track above. This is joined at a fine cairn.

Here starts a high traverse along the side of Swaledale. Sometimes this is in the open, with wooded outcrops of Applegarth Scar and Whitcliffe Scar above, the silver Swale below, and Swaledale views both before and behind. Sometimes it's in the green depths of a wood. Either way, it's a fine final runout to Richmond.

APPLEGARTH SCAR: The track runs down-valley, to pass below West Applegarth. Now it bends uphill, and here leave it, to slant down a few paces to the gable end of a barn. Pass below this barn, and go forward on the same level across two fields. Cross the tarred access track of Applegarth (not on map), and contour on to join the tarred lane leading towards East Applegarth (this lane is also not on the OS strip-map).

Stay on this lane just long enough to pass through a wall gap, then take a stile on the left. Pass along below a stone enclosure to a stile that leads onto a

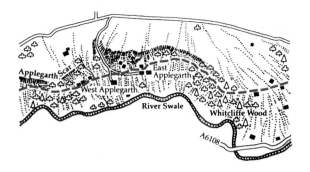

green track. This runs above East Applegarth, and joins a clearer track. This is positively the last farm called Applegarth. Now all is straightforward. The track leads on through Whitcliffe Wood, and becomes road at Whitcliffe Farm. Now it drops down the hillside, to join the main Reeth road at the outskirts of Richmond.

Keep ahead (Cravengate) where the main road bends left, to enter the next street on the left, which is the broad and elegant Newbiggin. At the Unicorn the street curves away left; here keep ahead to reach the Market Square.

Section 9
Vale of Mowbray

There comes a point in any serious enterprise when you've been at it so long you can't remember the beginning, but the end doesn't get any closer; your rucksack has worn a groove in your shoulder; and your feet hurt. For many, that low point in the walk will coincide with its physical low point. The Vale of Mowbray lies entirely below the 100m contour. Some people are excited by oilseed rape, and the various stages in the collapse of a ramshackle shed. For the rest, there are just two slightly better moments in the Vale of Mowbray. The first is the misprinted gravestone at Bolton-on-Swale. The second is the White Swan at Danby Wiske – and even there, the old-brick exterior is less interesting than the inside, where the beer is.

There are two routes, corresponding with the two ways of dealing with the Vale of Mowbray. You can put your feet in some trainers and your head down, and do the roads: eight miles (13 km) of roads, with a brief break around Streetlam. Or you can do the field paths. The field paths work: the stiles are there, and the waymarks, and the ditches have plank bridges hidden among the thorn bushes. And the effort of finding all this will keep you alert and interested.

The Pennines take a while to peter out. At first there's a riverside, and the river's still the Swale, and there are steep banks and a final flowery wood, the twelfth of the journey. Even after you've crossed the A1 at Catterick and left the Swale for ever, there's that implausible tombstone at Bolton, and a buttercup brook for a mile or two

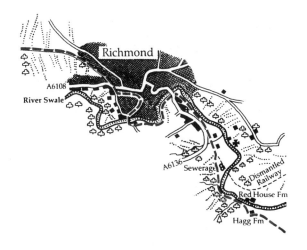

or 3km) beyond. The Vale starts at Ellerton Hill, and here you must choose your strategy. The road is slightly quicker. The fields are slightly less uninteresting.

Thirteen miles later you reach Ingleby Cross. Its sandstone church is oddly reminiscent of the one at Bolton-on-Swale; they have the same yellow stone, the same yews growing out of the churchyard. What a shame they could not be the same place!

DIFFICULTIES: Grassland paths to Catterick not well marked. Croplands on the off-road alternative, and also at Wray House and Sydal Lodge: tricky stile-finding when dry, muddy trench when wet.

RICHMOND to INGLEBY CROSS, 22 miles (33km): 500 ft (200m). GOING: easy.

Leave the Market Square at its south-east corner, next to the Talbot Inn. New Road leads to The Bar, a narrow pedestrian street on the left. The stone arch at the end is an original postern gate in the town walls, giving access to the bridge below for pedestrians and packhorses (which category is the Coast-to-Coast walker?).

From the postern a steep cobbled street (Cornforth Hill) descends to the Green. Richmond Bridge is ahead. 50m/yds past the bridge, a footpath on the left (Toilets) leads back to the riverbank, with a fine view up the castle walls on the other bank. The path rises through a wood, and drops back to the riverbank for Station Bridge.

The Devil himself built the first bridge over the Swale: and never got paid for it. The agreed fee had been the soul of the first living being to cross the bridge – but a Swaledale shepherd had arranged in advance for his dog to be ferried across the river, and whistled it back across the new arch.

The satanic bridge was swept away in the flood of 1771. There was a dispute as to who should replace it – not surprising, given that the builder of the original bridge was still waiting for his pay. In the end, the county built the southern half of the bridge, and three years later, the corporation built the town end.

Richmond Bridge and Station Bridge are referred to locally as Green Bridge and Mercury Bridge (Richmond currently having two different bridges, and no station).

STATION BRIDGE: Go under the bridge, and up

steps on the right to the road. Turn left, to pass between the swimming pool and the former station, now a garden centre. Behind the station is the start of the former railbed, now a municipal path, exceedingly green and shady. After 800m/yds, a cattle grid leads out onto the access track to the nearby sewage works. (Signs offer an emergency phone – for those Coast-to-Coast walkers who incautiously climb over the high fence and fall into the sewage?).

Follow the hedge round to right of the sewage works to the riverbank. A stile leads into a wood of the mud-and-wild-garlic sort. After two footbridges, the path climbs to give a view across to the ugly roofs of Red House Farm – we have now left the National Park, and scenic beauty will be permitted only when it doesn't get in the way of anything important.

The path leaves the wood and follows the top of the wooded bank to pass to the right of a barn conversion (Hagg Farm). The stony track ahead leads downhill to a gate with signpost.

Note carefully the direction of the signpost: people go astray here. A faint path leads up the field beyond, south-east, towards a skyline power pole. (Some field boundaries here, marked on the map, no longer exist.) A stile at the top leads to the next field. Again, this is crossed south-east, diagonally left.

A final stile leads into a large field crossed by power lines (two sets). Follow the left-hand side of the field to its bottom corner. A stile leads left to the streamside path, and thus to the driveway before COLBURN HALL.

Cross a small bridge into the village. The street leads past the Hildyard Arms. Where it bends right, go forward 20m/yds to a Coast-to-Coast sign. This points right, into the farmyard.

On the right is a semicircular annex built onto a barn. This pantiled, arched stone structure is a horse-gang: horses walking round a capstan would operate, by way of an endless belt, various sorts of machinery in the main building. Hollins Farm, Swaledale, had one too.

Turn left at the end of the farmyard onto a field track, and left at the end of the second field. Tractor wheelmarks beside the hedge lead to the top of the banking above the river's flood plain. From here to Catterick the route, not well-trodden, will follow this bank top.

Take the right-hand edges of two long narrow fields, and pass well left of St Giles' Farm to a stile beside white gates, to follow the farm's access track for 40m/yds. Where the track bends right, follow the field edge on the left, thus keeping to the top of the flood plain banking for a sudden look down into the Crow Hole. After another 400m/yds, a track runs up from the left and leads forward to Thornbrough Farm. Here step through a gap in barbed wire on the left, to go down the banking to the riverside and pass through the echoing cave of the A1's road bridge. (Did the concrete for the bridge come, as we have done, from Shap cement works?)

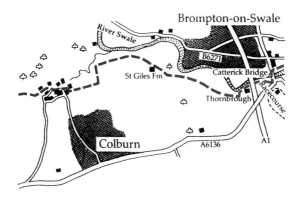

Pass under the former railway bridge, and turn diagonally away from the river to cross the overflow car park for Catterick Racecourse. Turn left to cross CATTERICK BRIDGE.

A stile at the end of the bridge parapet leads down to the riverbank. Follow this, overhung by willows, for almost a mile (more than a kilometre). With the ugly gravel works visible ahead, a sign points slightly left across the field to a red gate at its far corner. This leads onto the road. Follow this for 300m/yds: dandelions on the right are some compensation for traffic on the left. A sign indicates a tarred lane on the right, and after another 300m/yds a gravel track leads left into the north end of BOLTON-ON-SWALE.

Bear left at the village pump, and pass through the churchyard to visit the tall pyramid that is the monument to the oldest dead man in England (perhaps). Henry Jenkins carried arrows at the battle of Flodden (1514), and died in 1670 having lived through the reigns of five kings, two queens and Oliver Cromwell.

Pass to right of the church to leave the churchyard at the end of the village. Just before the small bridge over the Bolton Beck, a footpath sign on the right points to a stile. Follow the beck downstream, on the right bank for the first half mile (800m), then crossing on a brick arch to follow the left bank. Cross the access track to Laylands Farm. The stream bank leads across a final field to the Danby Wiske road. Turn left.

ELLERTON HILL: Those wishing to go forward by the slightly quicker, rather than the slightly less boring route, will follow this road for 3 miles (4.5km) to Streetlam. They will cross the larger road to a footpath sign in front of the phone box, and follow this due east, mostly along hedges, to join the access track of Middle Farm. This track will return them to the road for the final ¾ mile (1 km) into Danby Wiske.

Slightly more interesting is the field route, which turns off right after 200m/yds onto the tarred lane in front of Ellerton Hill (bridleway arrow, not footpath arrow to left). At the end of the buildings, go forward past the wall-end. The hedge on the left leads down to a gate between high thorns. The B6271 road is just beyond.

The road leads left, past Kiplin Hall. This handsome

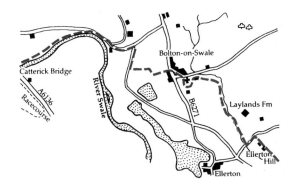

mansion, built of warm orange brick to a design by Inigo Jones, offers a real moment of pleasure during the flat crossing. The grounds are open always, the house with its lake and garden on Wednesdays and Saturdays.

Pass a minor road to Whitwell and Forest, and enter the track to Ladybank House on the left. At the two small houses, a narrow, overgrown track leads ahead between thorn bushes to a waymarked gate.

Take the footpath ahead, not the bridleway left. Tractor wheelmarks lead along the edge of a field with plantation on the right, to the gap at the end of a cross-hedge. Continue with the hedge on the right to a waymarked wooden gate. Now with the hedge on the left, go uphill, through a metal gate, to a ruin just over the brow of the hill. Stanhope Cottage was once a fine little brick house, with an arched doorway.

Pass to left of the ruin, and descend with a hedge on the left to a track bridge over a ditch and a way-marked gate. Follow the hedge on left, then keep ahead across the field towards a pair of trees, to find a hedge corner with a misleading waymark. The hedge ahead leads to a gate at the corner of the B6271.

Turn back sharp left (bridleway sign) on the track to Red House. At the two farms turn right at a foot-path waymark into Moor House farmyard. A gate leads round to the right of the farm buildings, through vile mud and around a blue cylindrical tank to a red gate. Go through the gate, and turn right (waymark, points north-east). Cross the field to a footbridge marked by a white post. Cross two more fields, eastwards, to another waymarked foot-bridge: steer by the power line that parallels your

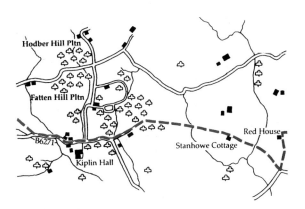

116

course some 100m/yds to the right. After this second footbridge, cross a short field end for 80m/yds to a white stile. Now follow the hedge on the left to a gate that leads onto the road opposite Middle Brockholme.

Turn right, down the road, for 400m/yds, and enter the access track for High Brockholme. Where this bends right towards the farm, go ahead through a waymarked double gate, and forward 80m/yds to a second gate. Go down a long field for 400m/yds with a hedge on the right, to a gate. Here footpaths cross, and waymarks are various and confusing.

Go through this multiple-waymarked gate, and turn left along the hedge for 30m/yds to a gateway ahead. Do not go through, but turn right along the hedge, to pass a low ruin hidden under high hawthorn.

Go uphill, eastwards. A hedge is on the left, and you pass under a low-voltage power line. At the top of the hill, a gate leads into a green lane between hedges so high they meet overhead. Follow this lane, ducking under barbed wire where a track cuts across. The lane ends at the top of a field.

Follow the hedge on the left until this ends after a few steps. Advance to the hedge opposite, and follow it downhill, in the direction of a skyline water tower. A stile leads out to road 500m/yds south of DANBY WISKE.

Leave the village on the Northallerton road, crossing the stream and then the railway bridge, to take

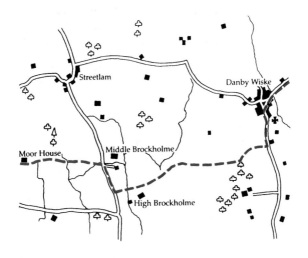

steps down left beside the tracks. Cross a short field
end and turn right along the hedge. Cross a ditch,
then a farm track, to a stile hidden in the field corner opposite the turkey barn of Lazenby Grange.
Still with the hedge on the left, and aiming for the
watertower ahead, walk under the power lines to
find a footbridge on the left. Cross, and turn right –
careful inspection will reveal this to be the downstream direction.

At the field end, turn up left for 100m/yds to a stile.
Cross the field beyond to a stile and white pole.
Diagonally left across the field is the grey gate on
Fox Covert Farm's entrance track. This track leads
out to the A167 opposite Lovesomehill Farm, with
its fox weathervane and camping barn.

LOVESOME HILL: Turn right (south) along the main road to a gate on the left, with a stile but no footpath sign. It leads to a wide track between hedges. Where this ends, the stile on the left leads to a field. Follow its right-hand hedge to the beginning of a green lane. This leads out to the next road, Deighton Lane.

Turn left up the verge for 100m/yds, and take the track on the right to Moor House. Take a concrete way ahead between the buildings, and turn left behind the barn to a gap at the wall corner. Go down to a stile, and follow a ditch round to a plank footbridge before Moor House Farm. Pass to right of the buildings.

A hedge on the left leads to a footbridge hidden in a thorn hedge. The corner is made more attractive by dog rose and enchanters' nightshade. Head

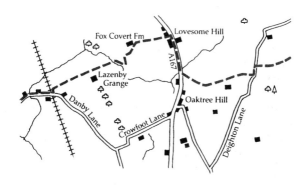

straight across the field beyond, to pass left of Northfield Farm onto the track beyond. This leads round to the right of Northfield House to the road beyond (Long Lane).

Go right, down the road, for 200m/yds, to the track on the left for Wray House. Waymarks point to the right in front of the house, through two gates and left along the end of an uncultivated garden to a ladder stile with a high sign warning of the perils of the railway. Tired walkers can reassure themselves by glancing down the line to the nearby level-crossing gates; if these are closed, it should be safe to cross.

Cross the following field eastward to another hidden footbridge. Follow the left-hand edge of the field, then turn right along its end at a Coast-to-Coast sign, to the tarred track beyond (Low Moor Lane).

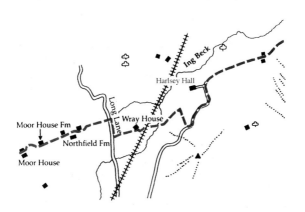

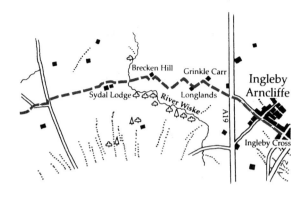

Turn left along the lane. It bends left, then right opposite Harlsey Grove. Ahead, the Cleveland Hills are now looking reasonably close: you can see individual trees at the top of Arncliffe Wood. After a mile (1.5 km), the lane is joined from the left by a minor road, and this runs forward to a T-junction.

Cross left between the brick gateposts of the track for Sydal Lodge. After the white gate, pass left of the buildings, to a waymarked gate. Now head across an open field towards the high chimneys of Brecken Hill, to pass a waymarked tree and find a footbridge concealed in a dip of the land.

The way passes to right of the ruined house onto a track. Follow this to the right, round bends, and turn left at Longlands Farm onto its gravel access track. At the end of this turn right onto the rough road that passes Grinkle Carr to reach the A19.

Cross the busy dual carriageway just south of the Little Chef and filling station. The road ahead leads into Ingleby Arncliffe. A fine tower, with no church attached, stands over on the right. Coast-to-Coast signs point the way through the village, left at the first junction and then right, for the last quarter-mile into Ingleby Cross. The Cross itself is a modern war-memorial but the Blue Bell is genuinely ancient, as is the small brick post office. Across the A19, the trees of Arncliffe Wood rise into the sky, and the Cleveland Hills run away for an indefinite distance into the north east.

Section 10
Cleveland Hills

I can't guarantee that as you cross the 100-metre contour at Arncliffe Hall the sun will come out and all your blisters suddenly heal up. But in every other way, things will become abruptly better – and stay better for the rest of the journey. You could start the count-down now: 51 miles to go. And not one among the 51 is a dull one, while the next 15 are very good indeed.

The way here is the Cleveland one which is, if anything, slightly over-engineered. Flagstones and pitched paths replace field edges, and there's never any problem finding the gap in the hedge. The map can go into the pocket, the guidebook into the sack. Relax, and enjoy the hills.

For they are enjoyable. Steep-sided, with rocky outcrops, they are variously patterned with bilberry, heather, bracken and grass. In places they are steep, but never steep for long. You may even be sorry, as you reach the tops of Cringle Moor and Hasty Bank, to find them passing beneath your feet so quickly. And Hasty Bank has the Wain Stones. Here you may be tempted to dangle off the surprising overhangs and pinnacles – it's one way to take the weight off your feet.

The beginning of the railway at Bloworth Crossing marks the natural end of the section, but sadly not the natural end to the day. The best accommodation Bloworth Crossing has to offer is a small heather tussock. B&Bs offer a pick-up-and-drop service from Clay Bank Top, but the nearest pathside beer, bed or tent space are at the Lion Inn, 5 miles (8km) into the following section.

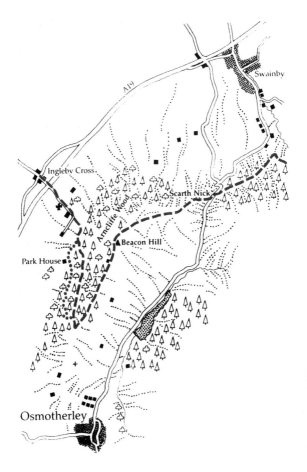

DIFFICULTIES: A lot of ascent and descent. Finding accommodation.

INGLEBY CROSS to BLOWORTH CROSSING,

15½ miles (25km): 3,400ft (1,000m). GOING: easy. BLOWORTH CROSSING IS NOT AN OVERNIGHT STOP. Ingleby Cross to Lion Inn, 21 miles (34km): 3,700ft (1,100m)

Take the short road down to the A19 and cross to the tarred lane opposite (No Through Road). It passes the small church, whose yellow sandstone matches the grander Arncliffe House beyond. For those with less highbrow taste, the garden opposite has a fine collection of historic gnomes.

The road bends right. Here a gate ahead (not the gate slightly left) has a small Coast-to-Coast sign and a larger one for Park House Adventure Centre. A track leads up to the gate at the foot of Arncliffe Wood. A forest road traverses right. After 250m/yds, and just before a stream, a muddy path strikes off left, and this can be taken to meet a forest road above and traverse right. (If the ground is wet, or you want the facilities of Park House, then stay on the lower road. It climbs gradually, finally doubling back left to meet the higher road at a Coast-to-Coast sign.) Immediately before the gate at the forest end, turn sharp back left into the forest.

To reach the very attractive village of Osmotherley with its chip shop and other facilities, go ahead through this gate onto a track with fine westward views. Above Chapel Wood Farm follow the upper, left, of two waymarked gates. Extra distance ¾ mile or 1.2km each way.

For the rest of this section the Coast-to-Coast coincides with the CLEVELAND WAY with its plentiful waymarks and signposts.

The wide pine-needle path heads up through the trees; occasional patches of hardcore hint at the less welcome aspect of the Cleveland Way – its reconstructed surface is harsh underfoot. The path reaches the top of the escarpment, with fine views out through birch trunks, across the top of the wood to the Vale of Mowbray with the Pennines looking a long, long way back. The fine views are interrupted by the passage behind the enclosure of the TV booster station, necessary if inhabitants of 'Heartbeat Country' are to watch *Heartbeat*. Here you pass between chainlink and a high wall.

As the path starts downhill, a gate on the right leads through the wall to a second gate, with stile. A stony track slants down, away from the trees, through heather. (A path next to the trees is an alternative.) After ¾ mile (1 km), drop to a wall just below the track on the left. A stepped path above the wall leads down to the road at Scarth Nick.

Cross the cattle grid below, to a gate on the right (no sign). The path traverses through woods to join a forest track above. After 600m/yds, hidden in bracken beside the path is the simple stone memorial to Bill Cowley, deviser and 'Chief Dirger' of the Lyke Wake Walk. Here a signed side-track heads down left to the gate at the bottom of the wood.

This gate leads out to Swainby, but turn right in front of it onto a wide path beside a hawthorn hedge. This runs along, not far above the bottom of the trees. Nettles, elder, and the hardcore path combine to make this wood one of the walk's gloomier ones.

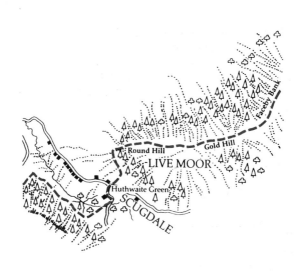

A Cleveland Way sign and stile point left, into an open field. The gate at the field's foot leads to a track through the stream, with a footbridge alongside, and then to the tarred lane. Follow this past Hollin Hill to the crossroads and phone box at Huthwaite Green.

For the whole of this section the Coast-to-Coast coincides with two older walks that helped bring it into being. The Lyke Wake Walk has its own feel and flavour, generated in part by its coffin emblem and its adoption of the beautiful, but not cheerful, Lyke Wake Dirge. The Dirge promises various torments: "the whinny moor, the Brig o' Dread, and rain that shall chill thee to the bare bane." These promises the walk fulfils, with deep and slippery peat making up many of its 45 miles (70km).

The 100-mile (160km) Cleveland Way was Britain's sec-

*ond National Trail (after the Pennine one). It is half moor-
land perimeter, half clifftop. Our route will coincide with
it again at Robin Hood's Bay, and these two samples give
a fair picture of the whole. While indebted to these two
ancestors, our route is more direct than the Cleveland Way,
happier than the Lyke Wake, and more varied than either.*

HUTHWAITE GREEN: Go straight across onto a
gravel footpath. This bends round left, to run along
the foot of the next of the escarpment-hung woods,
then turns sharply right for the steep climb through
the wood on pitched path, crossing a forest road on
the way up. It emerges onto open hill at the foot of
the ridge to Live Moor.

The clear path runs straight up the ridge and over
the crest of Live Moor. It passes slightly left of Gold
Hill, onto a heathery long ridge, with one or two
birch trees spotted at random onto the bleak
brown. The way is marked, if further mark were
needed, by small standing stones. As it climbs
Faceby Bank it passes a cluster of gregarious waymark poles at the top of the slope, and runs past the
Gliding Club on scraped bedrock.

*The group of upright shapes on Carlton Bank consists of
a cairn (modern); trig point (1930s); standing stone
(17th century); and erosion control notice (1990s).*

The path descends the rocky spur east, avoiding
falling over the edge of shaly mine workings on the
left; then is diverted in a long zigzag out to the
right.

GREEN BANK: Cross the road, and pass round to

left of the car park by a clump of evergreens. Here is a pointed boulder, one of the 'Lord Stones', of which the interpretation board, in some perplexity, can say only that they're a typical example of an archaeological remain. Turn into the car park for the cafe and water fountain: otherwise, advance to a signpost at the fence corner. The path leads across the col, passing to right of a small plantation around a pond. Take the right-hand gate – the path on the left bypasses Cringle Bank.

The bypass path, an old miners' track, isn't a right of way, but features in a NYMNP leaflet obtainable at the cafe. It offers better views of the Cringle Cliffs, and less good views of distant industrial Middlesbrough, and tired walkers may prefer it.

The grass path becomes gravel and climbs to the viewpoint on the high corner of Cringle Bank. After a fairly long stop to admire the view, it turns right along the edge. As it bends round left with the escarpment, the small path ahead, leading to the summit cairn and tumulus of Cringle Moor, is not a right of way. The true path follows the edge round, and drops down the rocky nose on the line of the OS map's pink dots.

Cross the grassy col with a wall on the right, to turn right through a gate, then left at a wall corner. Ahead, the west face of Broughton Bank is grassy, and shows a cave at half-height. The east faces of all the hills, on the other hand, are bracken and bilberry, while heather grows across the tops.

The summit of Broughton Bank boasts a tiny cairn.

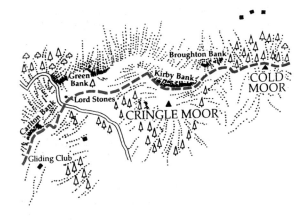

The path descends on flagstones, to cross the grassy col beyond through wall gaps and ascend the grassy slope to the Wain Stones. Here it makes its way up between the unstable-looking rock towers. They may be as unstable as they look, as they were named for their resemblance to a horse-and-cart, and this they don't resemble today. Those who like a scramble can leave the path and attempt an ascent slightly round to the right. 'DD' has carved his initials into the bottom of one attractive line.

The crossing of Hasty Bank continues along the top of a rock outcrop, with overhangs at various points. Again following pink dots on the OS strip-map, it drops to a stile at the side of the wood for the final 150m/yds down to Clay Bank Top.

These various road passes lead through to Bilsdale and Ryedale, the hidden valleys at the heart of the North York Moors. This country lay long undisturbed by the outside world; Bilsdale was known as 'abroad', so seldom were its inhabitants seen outside their valley. William the Conqueror came in 1076 intending to lay the place waste, but found it waste already. He did manage to get into Bilsdale but had the greatest difficulty getting out again. Many of his followers perished in a snowstorm at the crossing of Clay Bank.

So while Roman soldiers, marauding Scots, pilgrims, monks and merchants came and went on the Great North Road, behind the hills life changed slowly. Hobgoblins were a nuisance here long after they'd left the rest of Yorkshire. One farmer loaded all he owned onto packhorses and left Farndale to escape his 'Farndale Hob'. On the road over the moor he met a friend: "What's thoo doin', George, flittin'?" "Aye lad, we're flittin'!" was the reply – from inside the butter churn that hung from the saddle of the lead pony. With a sigh, the churn's owner turned back to Farndale.

If anywhere in Britain, then here in the hidden valleys of the moors the Gabbleratchet still flies by night, while at ground level crawl and slither the Gytrash and the spectral Bargest. Kirkdale is your best bet for a rare sighting of the Loftus Worm.

From the remedies against witches, monsters and other difficulties, these are of particular benefit along the Coast-to-Coast:

* Against cramp: wear a ring made of lead from a long-buried coffin
* Against other bodily aches: rainwater from a church roof, particularly from the chancel
* If a bootlace should come loose, walk on nine paces

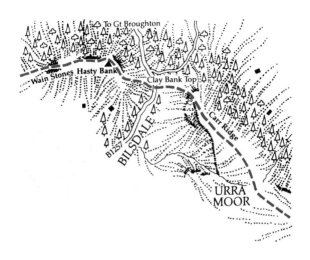

before retying it, else you'll tie in bad luck
* To mollify hobs and fairies, leave food and cash (not credit cards) in the small hollow on Ralph Stone, just past the Lion Inn in the next section.

CLAY BANK TOP: Cross the road to a gate, and go up with trees to the left. The clear, well-built path becomes a broad track, up the long Carr Ridge: it follows the OS strip-map's pink dots, which are now also the right of way line. Many small boundary stones mark the way.

At the path's high point, a more peculiar stone stands beside the track. It resembles a person with a square head, no neck, and no arms or legs either, and is the 'Hand Stone'. Here a short branch-path runs off to the left to the trig point on Round Hill. This is the high point of the Clevelands, and indeed the highest point anywhere east of the Pennines. The view northwards is given sparkle by the silly little spike of Roseberry Topping, known as the "highest hill i' all Yorkshire"!

Return to the main track for another mile (1.5 km). As it starts to descend, ignore a green track branching left and stay on the main stony one. It degenerates into a boggy trail, then rises to join the track running along the former ironstone railway. Turn right, through (or round the end of) a gate to a signpost. Here the Cleveland Way leaves us, turning back sharply left – it simply can't resist that Roseberry Topping.

Section 11
North York Moors

Again the route finding is easy, and now the walking is too: continuously downhill for 18 miles (28km) from Round Hill to Glaisdale Station. On broad, stony tracks – some of them are ancient roads – the way crosses the wide heather. The scenery is purplish-brown, black where it's been burnt down for grouse, decorated with little standing stones that are 18th century waymarks. On either side, green valleys of cultivation bite deep into the high plateau like brightly coloured maggots wriggling into a brown fruit.

The six miles to the Lion Inn are on the railbed of the old ironstone railway. It could be a bit monotonous, but for the constantly changing views as the trackway dips in and out of the re-entrants at the head of Farndale. Beyond the Lion, road alternates with peaty trod, but the standing stones here are really weird. (A vigorous short cut through Rosedale is offered, at the end of this section, for those who don't like roads.) There's a sudden view into Great Fryup; the valley-maggot here has rock teeth at its biting end.

The last long track runs out along Glaisdale Rigg. The side views are into Glaisdale itself and Eskdale. The stony way is busy with walkers, reminding of days when pilgrims made their way to Whitby Abbey, and monastic sales reps carried their samples behind them on a pack-pony.

DIFFICULTIES: none.

BLOWORTH CROSSING to GLAISDALE, 15$^{1}/_{2}$

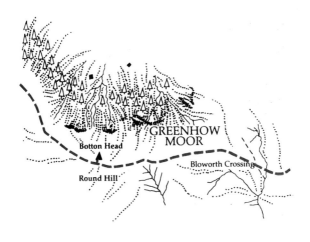

miles (25km): 600ft (200m). GOING: easy. Lion Inn to Glaisdale, 10 miles (16km): 300ft (100m)

The railbed passes through a second gate and runs eastwards round the head of Farndale. Walk on it for 5½ fast miles (9 quick kilometres). In the cuttings, damp trickles on the track are stained orange. Ten million tons of iron-rust was carried out along this railway, but more is still leaking out of the bog. After offering various views into the head of Farndale, the line contours into a col; on this embankment it also offers a new view northwards into Eskdale.

A path ahead is the former route of the Lyke Wake Walk, but is blocked by signs saying that it's 'closed for reseeding'. This closure has now allowed time for the reseeded plantlife to grow, if it wished, to head-height. However, don't let's disparage the

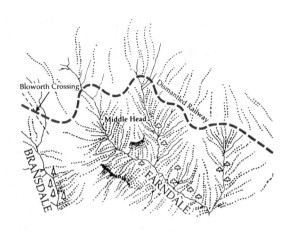

possessiveness of grouse-moor owners. The Lyke-Wake short cut, if permitted, would shorten this enjoyable high walking and bypass the very necessary convenience of the Lion Inn.

From the final cutting we see a fresh landslip on the valley wall opposite, and the Lion Inn perched on the brow above. The railway curves round the head of the last re-entrant to a small cairn marked LWW in white paint. The inn is no longer visible, but a path strikes up left to a stone wall beside a stone-and-pantile hut. (Or continue ahead, for the vigorous Rosedale short cut described at the end of the section.)

Go up beside the stone wall and to the right at its corner, to a tumulus finished off with an upstanding boundary stone. The hollow in the top of this was the work of gentlemanly grave-robbers, and was then put to use by their proletarian contemporaries for holding illegal cockfights in. The cheerful pantiles of the Lion are just ahead.

LION INN: From the tumulus the way turns back left and drops to the tarred road. Follow this, away from the inn, for a mile (1.5km) to a particularly impressive standing stone (Margery Bradley) on the left. A path drops off the roadside on the right, signed with the fish emblem of the Esk Valley Walk. It heads north-east, following boundary stones – on the map, this is the line of the boundary, not the marked bridleway. The path climbs in a direct line to White Cross – another standing stone with white top at the roadside.

White Cross is also known as 'Fat Betty': it and Margery Stone commemorate the wanderings of the prioresses of Rosedale and Baysdale, lost here in mist while settling a boundary. Ralph, whose two stones stand nearby, was their unhappy guide. Presumably the two stones are witty caricatures of the two good ladies.

Follow the road to right for another ¾ mile (1.4 kilometres) to a footpath pole-sign on the left. This indicates a peaty trod through the heather which shortcuts to a northward side road. Turn left, for 600m/yds, to a wide gate on the right with wicket gate alongside. Down the stony track ahead you can see the rooftop of Trough House.

The valleys below us now were not always so green and pleasant. When man first arrived after the ice age they were dreadful places, sodden and overgrown with thorns, and the first settlements were here on the tops. The land-scape was progressively tamed by agricultural monks, and they, too, developed in early Tudor times the local industrial base, mining the hills for coal, ironstone, alum and jet. At the same time they built their well-proportioned abbeys and priories – and kept on building them, whenever the Scots came and burnt them down.

On this walk we have passed their settlements at St Bees and at Shap; at Marrick, Richmond and Easby; and at Mount Grace under Beacon Hill. Some remained austere: at Mount Grace the friars received their food through an angled hatchway so as not even to see the fellow-human who served them. Others became fat: Wycliffe railed against the wealth of the 'poor friars' of Richmond. Either way, it is to them we owe the shape of the landscape today: – the walled lanes of Shap; the hanging woods and grey field barns of Swaledale; and the green hollows below the North York Moors.

In 1636-9, in an act of wholesale privatisation, Henry VIII handed the monasteries over to the feudal aristocracy and the newly-discovered Middle Class.

TROUGH HOUSE offers only the shelter of its outside walls. The drips off the corrugated roof ensure you don't linger too long. Beyond the house the track becomes a mud hollow, and after a few steps comes the sudden view down into Great Fryup. Nutrition for long-distance walking, we're told, should be based on complex carbohydrate: the only recommended way to enjoy a Great Fryup is from this path, as you gaze down into its sudden and sombre depths.

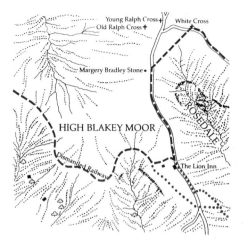

The path is muddy and stony as it circles the head of the valley. The crags opposite are small but surprisingly grim, blackened by the peat that drips down their faces. The rectangular standing stones beside the path are the least cheerful decoration imaginable. The path turns north-east around the head of the valley, and after a mile (1.5km) emerges onto the moorland road. 60m/yds down the road, another lumpy stone lies in the heather while offering an inscrutable message on its uphill side.

The road continues gently downhill for another mile (1.5km), passing an upstanding cairn on the right (path but no right of way to visit this). Just before the trig point at the top of Glaisdale Rigg the road bends left, and a wide stony track continues ahead, marked 'Unsuitable for Motors'.

This track runs straight down the long ridge. It

crosses a diagonal cross-track marked by standing stones. Just before this, a stone on the left indicates that this was formerly the Whitby Road, and in our day, again, the moor top provides the easy trouble-free way. Bridleways branch off, but they are mere green strips through the heather.

The ridge-end dips more sharply, and is joined from the right by a fence. At a gate it becomes a tarred lane leading down into the north end of Glaisdale. Turn right towards the village, and note the path descending to right of the Robinson Institute: this will be our way out. But first, we probably want to visit the extremely convenient Convenience Store and Post Office ahead.

VARIANT: ROSEDALE HEAD

800m/yds shorter but 500ft (150m) more ascent. Most walkers agree that roads aren't what walking's all about. And then, when the choice arises, it's raining and we want our tea, we take the road. This short cut through Rosedale interrupts the rather spiritless downhill trickle of 18 miles (almost 30km) from the top of Round Hill to Beggar's Bridge. It lets you experience one of the green hollows you've been looking down into from the railway. It eliminates three miles (4.5 km) of road. Afterwards, you'll regret that you didn't take it.

From the Lion Inn, take the road south for 500m/yds. A track leads down left. (Or ignore the Lion, follow the railway to its end at a road junction, and cross to a footpath sign 'Rosedale' to go down grassy slopes to the same track.) Follow the

track down, to go through the gate before Moorlands Farm.

Go left through gate to Hollin Bush Farm. Go down
in front of this to a gate, but not through the gate.
Take the through-stone stile immediately to its
right, and go down to the middle of the bottom of
the field below. Here are oak trees, and a footbridge
hidden in the dip.

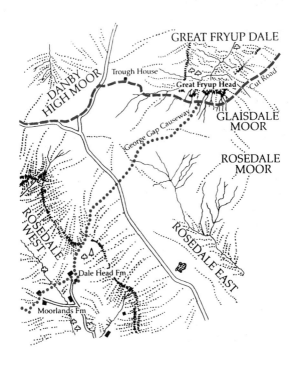

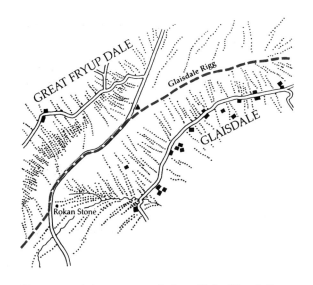

Slant up right, to gate below Dale Head Farm
(strictly, the eastern one of two Dale Head Farms).
Go up right, to a second gate (no field boundary
below) onto the tarred farm road. Go up the road
for 10m/yds to a bridleway signpost 'Great Fryup
Dale' opposite. Go round to the right of all the farm
buildings, to a path above a wooded stream. This is
steep, green and pretty.

It meets a track emerging from a field on the left,
and runs to the right through a gate and above a
new plantation to reach another abandoned
railbed. The two bridleways ahead are deep
grooves with streams in. Today's path runs up to
left of the main stream, and as the slope eases,
crosses it to a conspicuous cairn. With a few more

cairns, the peat path crosses the moor to meet a road at a bridleway pole.

The bridleway opposite starts as a wet track, but declines to a peat path. As it crosses the moor top, it becomes an ancient paved way. It crosses the deep peaty hole of the Lyke Wake Walk at a clump of boundary stones: one of them is the white-topped 'Causeway Stone'.

The path bends slightly right at this point, becoming indistinct, though stretches of causeway still appear among the rushes. Two guiding signposts also help in clear weather. You should reach the Cut Road path at a cairn with bridleway signpost planted in it.

Section 12:
Eskdale and the Sea

Eastern Cleveland is much better than western Cumbria. Cosy green valleys run out from the moorland to the sea. Eskdale is the first stretch of the walk that could be described as 'charming', even as 'sweet'. It has a pretty little stone-arch bridge down in the woods. It has a pretty little river with stepping stones over. It has a pretty little steam railway.

In case this is just too much sweetness, two final arms of the moor provide a last taste of heather and peat. Between them, the last valley is little – indeed, Little is its name – but not altogether pretty. The way edges through steep trees above the ruined hall, the gritstone waterfall. It's a reminder of days when we took to the tops because the bottoms were too grim and impenetrable: days when we were scared of getting lost in the woods.

At St Bees it was pink sandstone: now it's ochre grit. At St Bees it was the Irish Sea, and now it's the North one. England has been crossed. Three miles (5km) of high, wild walking lead to the little town, jammed between its cliffs, its streets running straight down into the sea.

DIFFICULTIES: the path across Sleights Moor is indistinct, with deep heather the penalty for straying. Short stretch of pathless heather after John Cross. Final clifftop is shelterless and exposed to weather.

GLAISDALE to ROBIN HOOD'S BAY, 21 miles (34km): 1,900ft (600m). GOING: easy/moderate.

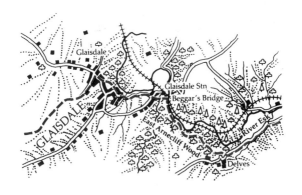

At the north (top) end of the village is the Robinson Institute. To the right of this building a tarred path descends, bending right to join a descending street. After a sharp left bend the street descends to the valley floor, soon to rejoin the major road above. The Arncliffe Arms is opposite.

Cross to a rough path that descends just left of the inn. After a footbridge, turn left on a track that runs down towards a ford with a white footbridge on the right. Just before this footbridge, a stepped path climbs steeply into the wood: this is the onward route, but first we take the footbridge and pass under the railway to inspect the Beggar's Bridge.

Beggar's Bridge is just the latest of various stone arches that have been a feature of the Coast-to-Coast. We recall the tree-hidden Parish Crag Bridge at the end of the Lake District, Frank's one at Kirkby Stephen and lonely Smardale Bridge crossed by its forgotten road. Beggar's

Bridge, trapped between the modern iron railway viaduct and the even more modern road bridge, isn't lonely at all; but it is the finest narrow high arch of them all, and also has a cafe beside it.

Mr Ferris, who built it, was not strictly speaking a beggar, though he was poor enough to own neither pony nor boat, and so was forced to visit his fiancee on the other side by paddling. Anyone who's crossed rivers in the dark, dressed in their girlfriend-visiting best, will understand why Mr Ferris promised himself that if he should ever get rich, he'd build a bridge across the thing. He did become rich, and indeed an alderman in the city of Hull, and so we have this elegant stone arch. It's a shame there is no way of re-routing the Coast-to-Coast so as to have to cross it.

BEGGAR'S BRIDGE: Return under the railway viaduct, re-cross the white footbridge, and take the steep stepped path that zigzags up into the wood above the river. The path drops back to the river-bank for 400m/yds. As the river bends left, the path goes ahead, climbing below the branches on ancient flagstones.

The wood is full of bilberry bush, wood sorrel and rocks, with the odd overhanging crag. Somewhere in here is a cave where Robin Hood used to lurk with all his men: what's more, they had a secret tunnel twenty miles long leading all the way to Robin Hood's Bay... Just before the top of the flags, a viewpoint on the left looks down on treetops and the railway bridge. Now broad and muddy, the way climbs gradually to meet the road above.

Turn left along the road. It descends steeply to the valley floor, where it crosses a ford with footbridge alongside. After another 200m/yds, fork left to pass the Horseshoe Hotel. Just before the road above, a sign 'Stepping Stones' points down left.

Take the path to the riverbank, and then downstream, passing under a white footbridge. The stepping-stones are high square blocks. They cross the river in two stages by way of an island. From the further bank, a tarred track leads between the houses into EGTON BRIDGE.

Turn right through the village to a T-junction. Here turn left and at once right into the stony track signposted 'Grosmont 1ml'. This leads past Egton Manor and under the railway, then past the former toll house. It's important to survive the journey at least this far: passing through dead and in a hearse

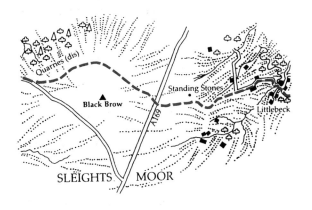

will cost you 6d in old money. At the Grosmont-Egton road a right turn leads across the river and back under the railway into GROSMONT.

Grosmont is pronounced by locals as 'Gro'mont'. In summer it's busy with passengers from the North York Moors Steam Railway, and even busier with visitors seeking the site of the TV series Heartbeat.

The main street leads past tempting cafes and over the level crossing of the steam railway. A signed path on the right is the diversion for those who wish to inspect the engines in their shed. Otherwise, follow the street until it bends left, when a sign ahead (for Goathland and Pickering) warns of 1 in 3 slopes. Indeed, the Fair Head Lane out of Grosmont is the eighth steepest climb of the entire walk (also, by coincidence, the eighth longest). The road levels, then turns right at a junction for an even longer climb that's 1 in 3 only to start with. At last, after a cattle grid, the road emerges onto open moorland.

Ignore the bridleway sign pointing along a track on the left, but follow the footpath sign pointing half-left just above. A sketchy path leads out into the heather, passing just above the orange shaly knolls that are the top of an abandoned quarry.

Now the path bends gradually right as it contours round the side of Black Brow. Ignore cross-paths descending to grouse butts below. The northern flank of the hill once rounded, the path slants gently downhill, to reach the A169 road at a wide gate. A large blue road sign, just below, indicates the start of Blue Bank, a steep descent.

Cross the road to another gate. Here heather may be seen stacked in giant bales for export to the Netherlands. (They use it to protect winter bulbs from frost.) A mud-and-grass track leads down the heather slope. On the left, a row of standing stones can be glimpsed, at the point marked 'sheep bield' on the OS map. A public footpath leads across to the stones, which boast a northward view with a bit of sea in it. Return along the same line to the track.

The track is joined from the right by a wider gravel one, and descends through a gate to the corner of the public road. This descends steeply, looking down onto the roofs of Littlebeck. A footbridge on the left lets you avoid the road's ford.

LITTLEBECK: A few yards up the road is a kissing-gate and bench on the right. This is the start of a path that goes upstream through woods on the steep bank of the beck. After 200m/yds, the path heads left, away from the main stream, around the head of a deep little side-valley. It returns to the right, to cross the roof of a small cave. After another pleasant 800m/yds it rises through the wood on stone steps, to reach the Hermitage.

This is a small chamber carved out of bedrock and marked above the doorway 'C + C 1790'. Has the Coast-to-Coast really been established so long – or is that second C, disappointingly, a G? Do not take the branch-path down right at the Hermitage but continue climbing slightly. In 80m/yds, take a right fork, horizontal, at a C to C waymark. Now open ground around Newton Farm is above the path.

500m/yds after the Hermitage, a second branch-path descends to the right, with another C to C waymark, and this one you do take. It runs across a steep slope of earth, trees and rocks, with a view to the waterfall of Falling Foss. The path slants down to reach the abandoned Midge Hall.

This was formerly a museum, but now stands abandoned in a dismal green shade below the wooded slopes. Immediately in front of the hall, a small path to the right can be taken for a close and rather risky glimpse over the brink of the fall. The main way goes to the left of the hall to a footbridge.

Cross the footbridge, and the track beyond. A muddy path leads up the right-hand bank of the stream for 50m/yds, then crosses it by leaping over

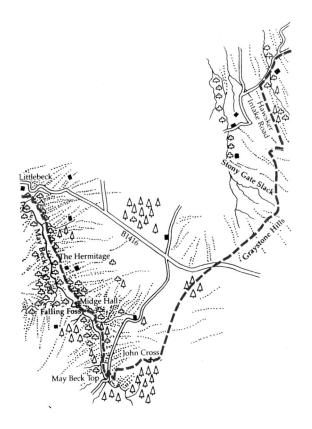

some stone slabs. (If the stream is too full for this, return to cross on the stone bridge used by the track.) After another 150m/yds, the path rises to join a larger one above. The path continues through the woods, with the stream not far below on the right, to emerge at a tarred track beside its bridge over the beck.

MAY BECK TOP: Turn sharp left, away from the bridge, and go up the road for 70m/yds. A single gatepost is on the left, and here a footpath sign points back sharp right. (This right of way has been diverted, and does not follow the line indicated on the OS map.)

The path crosses a fence by a stile, and slants up right for 100m/yds to a signpost with a view ahead into a scrubby ravine (the Blea Hill Beck). Here it doubles back to the left, to rejoin the fence. It turns uphill, with the fence on its left, to a stile, and straight up the field above alongside a broken wall to a ruin. A stile just above leads out beside the north-west corner of a wood. Head up leftwards to join a track. This goes up to a gate, reaching the open moor at the top corner of the same wood.

JOHN CROSS is a plain stone post standing in a hollowed-out plinth. Turn left, alongside the wall on the left, on a small path. Boundary stones stand alongside the wall, and a footpath turns off left but is ignored. 800m/yds after the Cross, slant away from the wall into a wood of scattered pines. The trees are twisted and old, and make enough shade so that there is grass, not heather, under them. Go straight through the wood, north-east. Rough heather beyond leads to a gate onto the B1416 road.

Cross the road to a gate opposite with footpath sign. The path ahead is narrow but clear through the heather, and marked with high waymark poles and signposts.

GRAYSTONE HILLS: The path traverses, keeping

parallel with the main road above. A descending track crosses it at a signpost. It now has some boggy bits, and a duckboarded section at the head of the Stony Gate Slack. 50m/yds later the path forks. The smaller, left-hand fork is the line of the right of way (not the OS map's pink dots), and leads to a gate with a high signpost.

A green path leads forward along a field of gorse. Fences converge from both sides, making it easy to find the waymarked gate in the field's narrow end. Without going through this, turn right, alongside a bank and fence, to another gate. The way, marked as a track on the map, is pathless.

At the end of the following field, a metal gate on the left leads into Hawsker Intake Road. This green lane with nettles becomes a well-used farm track and leads out to the Hawsker road. Here turn right.

The road looks north to see Whitby Abbey. It drops into a wooded dip, and ignores a side road to Low Hawsker, then bends left at a stream. After another 100m/yds, a footpath sign points left. Follow it to a stile just left of buildings, and along the right edge of a field to the main road. The footpath continues across the road, to reach the main street of HAWSKER.

Leave the village at a bridleway sign on the right immediately north of the Hare and Hounds. After 200m/yds the track crosses above the abandoned coastal railway, then leads on to Gnipe How – with only sea visible behind the buildings. Take a way-marked gate on the right, before the farm, and fol-

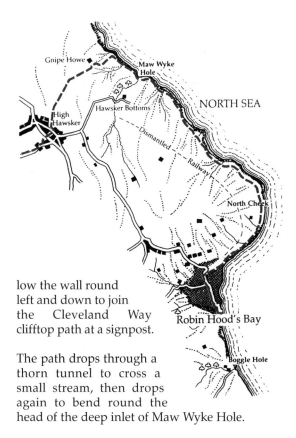

low the wall round left and down to join the Cleveland Way clifftop path at a signpost.

The path drops through a thorn tunnel to cross a small stream, then drops again to bend round the head of the deep inlet of Maw Wyke Hole.

The broad, well-signposted coastal path runs on along the clifftop. This seacliff is gradually eroding, and it is most advisable to obey the signposts and be wary of small paths closer to the edge.

At Normanby Stye Batts, the way shortcuts across a

small headland and is unclear on the short grass; in thick sea-mist it's easier to grope round by the wall on the left. 400m/yds later, it jinks inland to negotiate a stream valley. At Cow and Calf, a stone wall beside the path has failed to obey 'Path Diversion' signs and has consequently fallen over the edge into the sea.

A white coastguard lookout above the path indicates the onset of the 191st mile of the walk. Through the blackthorn thickets that protect the seaward side of the path, the houses of Robin Hood's Bay appear. At Rocket Post Field there used to stand a ship's mast mounted on dry land for firing rockets at and practising bosun's chair manoeuvres. A board explains the local geology.

The path becomes a gravel way along the fronts of houses, and then a street (Mount Pleasant North). At the main road, turn down left to a car park, and then on down the steep street ahead.

Just before the street crosses a small stream, turn off left. Chapel Street is a paved walkway barely wide enough for a rucksacked Coast-to-Coast walker to pass a colleague just starting the backward journey to St Bees. At the street end, turn down King Street. This descends to become a slipway running down into the sea.

Do rinse the salt water out of your boots straight away. You will want those boots again. Unlikely as it may now seem, you're very soon going to start thinking about your next long-distance walk.

East to West 1:
Cleveland

ROBIN HOOD'S BAY: From the slipway, head slightly right up King Street, and left into the narrow walkway Chapel Street. At its end turn uphill, past the car park, then right into Mount Pleasant North. The street leads to a gravel path, which becomes the clifftop path.

After 3 miles (5km), a sign points up left (Hawsker) into a caravan site. Ignore. After another 800m/yds, a second Hawsker sign points left. A field edge leads to the left of Gnipe How onto its track. This leads into HIGH HAWSKER.

A path starts just south of the Hare and Hounds, to reach the Sneaton Thorpe road. After a wooded stream, at the brow of a hill, a farm track goes off left (Hawsker Intake Road). It becomes a green lane. At its end turn right, along the field-edge bank, to a waymarked gate on the right. Turn left (not through this gate) along a narrow field to a gate with a high signpost. A narrow, wet path, with high poles and signposts, leads across Graystone Moor.

Across the B1416 is a stile with a footpath sign. This points across pathless heather into a wood of twisted pines. Go through the wood to meet a wall on the right. Follow this, ignoring the first public footpath off to the right, to the gate and signpost at John Cross. The Cross is a remnant of stone stump alongside.

The right of way now differs from what's on the map. It follows the track on the right, through its gate, and half-way down the first field to a small waymark. Now it descends left, to a stile at the bottom corner of the field. Cross a stile to a ruin, and go down the ruined wall beyond. A stile leads onto rough hillside. Go down beside fence, then follow signs left and back right, to join the road just above the car park at May Beck Top.

Go down a clear, signed path to right of the stream. Where this forks after 800m/yds, take the lower, left-hand one, to reach a ford in 150m/yds. (If impassable, stay on the right bank to the bridge below.)

The path crosses a track (ignore its bridge on the right) and takes a footbridge to the abandoned Midge Hall. Here take the lower of two broad paths ahead. Below and behind is the fine Falling Foss waterfall. The path rises to join another. After the rock-hollowed Hermitage, this descends on steps to rejoin the stream. Finally it reaches the tarred road at LITTLEBECK.

Turn left, crossing the stream. The road climbs, then bends right: take the track ahead, marked by a bridleway pole. After a gate, this becomes untarred and bends left. Take a lesser track of mud and grass, directly uphill. This reaches the main A169 beside a sign warning of the steep perils of Blue Bank.

Go straight across, onto a small bridleway path through heather. This starts off west, then contours round the hill above grouse butts. Pass above the beige hillocks of a disused quarry, to join the hill road above a cattle grid. Descend steeply into GROSMONT.

The road goes straight through this charming village, across the level crossing of the steam railway. Ignore the ford and footbridge on the left, and cross the road bridge. At once a sign points left down a gravel track (Egton Bridge). At the track end, turn left and immediately right into EGTON BRIDGE (past toilets). After 200m/yds, a sign points left to the stepping stones. Cross these, and turn right past the Horseshoe Hotel.

The road crosses a ford (footbridge alongside), then climbs towards Delves. Before this house, a signed path leads down right into muddy but delightful woodland. There are many paths, but the main one is the widest, and becomes an ancient paved way to reach the river below. It climbs again, then descends in zigzags to the clump of bridges at Glaisdale Station.

Beggar's Bridge is not on the route, which here turns left onto a track rather than crossing footbridge or ford on the right. The track bends right to a different footbridge, and goes up to the road at the Arncliffe Arms. Cross to the minor road ahead (Local Traffic Only). This turns steeply uphill, with a footway on the right. Turn off right, just above the antique 'Road Narrows' sign, onto an earth path. After a few metres it becomes tarred, to reach the road above. The shop and other village facilities are down to the left, while the Coast-to-Coast turns right.

GLAISDALE: At the north end of the village, a tarred lane turns back left and climbs to a grove of bridleway signs. Keep ahead, through a gate, on a gravel track that follows the top of Glaisdale Rigg. Bridleways branching off are all green and grassy: after 2 miles (3km) another gravel track is crossed diagonally. The track runs into moortop road. Continue climbing gently for another mile (1.5km).

An odd stone on the left (Rokan Stone) is followed after 80m/yds by gates on the right. Go through, and follow the path on the left (not the wheelmark-track ahead). This is the Cut Road, very clear and well-trodden, which circles the head of Great Fryup Dale with nice views down into it.

The track bends right (west), and passes a large cairn on the right, then dips to cross a stream. Here a small cairn on the left has a bridleway sign planted in it. Turn off left (across a short duck-board). The George Gap Causeway is small and indistinct, marked by two high signposts (not enough), then becomes an ancient paved way across the moor top. Heading south-west, it crosses the gouged trough of the Lyke Wake Walk at the white-topped Causeway Stone.

The path crosses a moor road at bridleway poles, to pick up a small stream. Cairns also mark its route. It crosses the head of a stream gully, and descends, to the right of the stream, to cross a former railbed. It continues as a track above a plantation to a field gate. Do not go through this, but take the green path downhill: the wooded stream on the left is lovely, as is the green end of Rosedale.

Dale Head Farm is the more easterly of two with this name. Go down the road below for a few steps, to a signed gate on the right. The right of way slants down to a footbridge concealed under trees, then up a narrow field to its top right corner. Go up the track to left of Hollins Farm, then left to Moorlands.

A watercourse-track leads up through a gate. It climbs to reach road 600m/yds south of the Lion Inn. Behind the inn turn left onto a path that descends alongside a stone wall to the trackbed of the former ironstone railway. Turn right, and follow this for 5 fast miles (8 quick kilometres). After a gate, the Cleveland Way joins from the right, and after another, it branches off left and we with it.

A wide gravel track crosses Round Hill: at the Hand Stone a short branch-off visits the trig at the high point of the North York Moors. The clear track continues, becoming gravelly path and then pitched path, which is one roughly-cobbled with adventitious rocks, as it descends to the road.

CLAY BANK TOP: The way across the Cleveland Hills is the eponymous Cleveland Way, which is built path and well signposted. Route description? "Follow the signposts and built path for 10 miles (16 km)." The Way rises over Cringle Bank, with the entertaining Wain Stones on the back slope, and then climbs over Broughton Bank and Cringle Moor with fine grit cliffs alongside on the right. The long view over the plains makes it all seem much higher up than 400m (1,300ft).

After the car park and semi-underground cafe at

Lord Stones, the Way climbs Carlton Bank and descends the long heathery ridge beyond. It drops steeply through a wood, then turns left along its bottom to HUTHWAITE GREEN.

The road opposite leads past Hollin Hill Farm to a track on the right, with a ford. A path leads up to the wood-bottom track. This runs along near the foot of Clain Wood, with a less well-marked branch track on the left as the only possible wrong turning. Beside a gate out of the wood, turn left, uphill, then right on a signposted track. This climbs, then traverses, through the wood. Where it bends left, a signed path leads ahead to a cattle grid on the Scarth Nick road.

Cross the grid to a path opposite. This goes up steps beside a wall, to join a track above. Follow this across the heather moor, or strike right to the edge of the trees. The main track enters the wood, and runs along its top: a delightful mile, apart from the few yards past the TV station. The path slants down through the wood to a gate at its end.

Here the Coast-to-Coast leaves the Cleveland Way, doubling back right on a forest road. Follow this as it traverses, ignoring a signed branch-track down left. A green track forks up right, which is not taken, but after another 200m/yds a path slants down left. Take this, to the track below. Turn right to the forest-end gate, and go through this down a field to the tarred lane before Ingleby church. Turn right, to cross the busy A172 into INGLEBY CROSS.

East to West 2:

Yorkshire

INGLEBY CROSS: Go straight through both Ingleby villages and cross the main A19 to a track. A waymark points left at Grinkle Carr and the muddy track continues, turning right at Longlands, to ruined Brecken Hill.

From the building's end, cross an open field just south of west to a hidden footbridge. (These field ways are obvious when trodden, but can be mystifying in spring and early summer.) Pass to the right of Sydal Lodge onto its track. Cross the tarred road leftwards to a branch road for Welbury. After 200m/yds, an unsurfaced road branches left, signed, simply, 'Coast'.

At the entrance to Harlsey Grove this bends left and becomes tarred. After further bends to right, left, and right, a stile on the right leads to a field path with hedge and fence on right. Turn left at the field corner, to find the footbridge (under thorns) of the Ing Beck. Cross the field beyond to the concrete ladder stile onto the railway.

The route round to left of Wray House is poorly waymarked in this direction. It goes through two gates (stiles alongside) onto the farm's access track. Turn right on Long Lane, and in 200m/yds the access track for Northfield leads left – the shortcut right of way is absent on the ground.

The waymarked route passes round left of North-

field House to a stile, and then right of Northfield Farm and across an open field (slightly south of west) to a footbridge in the hedge. Pass to the left of Moor House Farm, and follow a ditch round to Moor House. A wall-end leads to the corner of a barn, and through on concrete to the farm's track. Turn left on Deighton Lane for 100m/yds, to a green lane on the right.

The lane ends at a stile; a field-edge, then a muddy way between hedges, lead to the road at OAKTREE HILL.

Turn right along the verge for 500m/yds to Lovesome Hill (Camping Barn, B&B). At the water tower, the track on the left leads towards Fox Covert Farm. The route follows, with one deviation, the right of way: the map's nearby footpath is illusory. At the gate one field short of the farm, cross the field half-left to a stile. Cross to a second stile, and follow the field-edge left to the stream. Follow the stream up to a footbridge under power lines.

A long field-edge on the right leads just north of Lazenby Grange, passing the end of its big turkey-barn, to the railway. Steps lead up onto the road bridge. Cross railway and stream into DANBY WISKE.

In the village turn left (Yafforth). After the church and moated grange, a signed field path goes through a gate on the right. At the top of the slope, cross a 20m/yds hedge-gap on the left to a way-marked gate under trees. This leads to a hedged green lane. When the lane ends, continue in the same direction downhill with a hedge on the right – a ruin is hidden under hawthorns at the bottom. Continue with a fence on the right to the field corner: the gatepost here has multiple waymarks, as rights of way cross. Turn left along the hedge for 40m/yds to a gate on the right. Go through, and up a long field. Gates lead onto the access track of High Brockholme.

Turn right on the road beyond, and left into field opposite Middle Brockholme (B&B). Follow a hedge on the right to a stile. A short (80m/yds) field end leads to a footbridge in the hedge. Cross three fields beyond, westward, to Moor House.

Go round to left of a blue tank to a muddy gate and the farm's access track. Turn left on the track beyond to a corner of the B6271. At once turn sharp back right on signed footpath with hedge on left. When the hedge turns away left, keep ahead across field to a single tree. A hedge joins from the right, and leads to a waymarked gate and footbridge. Follow the hedge on the right to the ruined Stanhowe Cottage (GR296977, marked but not named on Land Ranger).

Continue past the house with hedge on the right and then on the left, to pass along the right-hand edge of a narrow plantation. A waymarked gate leads into a larger wood. The green lane is encroached on by thorns, but soon becomes a wide driveway. Turn right along the verge of the B6271 to Kiplin Hall. The grounds are open, and it's worth the short diversion to pay respects to this fine piece of architecture.

After another 500m/yds of the road, just before a brick-sided bridge, a bridleway leads off right. It follows the right-hand edge of a field up to Ellerton Hill. Turn left in the lane beyond, and right, just before the bridge of the Bolton Beck, onto a footpath.

The path takes fields alongside the beck, then crosses by a brick arch. Now with the brook on its right, it leads to BOLTON-ON-SWALE. Go through the churchyard and round left of the church to find the tall obelisk commemorating the implausibly long-lived Henry Jenkins. From the church gate cross to pass the pump and leave the village northwards.

At village end a lane on the left turns right at a T-junction to the B6271. Turn left past the gravel works to a gate leading down to the Swale. The crossing of the flat country may be considered complete. Follow the Swale bank to Catterick Bridge.

Cross the bridge, and go through the racecourse car park to rejoin the river. Go under the A1, and take a muddy path up left into a farmyard (Thornbrough). The bank just climbed is the edge of the Swale's flood-plain. The 2 miles (3km) to Colburn, along field-edges with confusing cross-tracks, is along the top of this banking.

Follow the track until it veers off right, down the banking. Field edges lead to the track before St Giles' Farm. Take a gate on the right before the farm, keeping a field's width to right of it past a waymarked power pole. Two narrow fields lead to a gate and stile before Colburn Wood. Tractor wheelmarks lead left along a field-edge to a farm track. Follow this right, through Colburn Farm, to COLBURN.

Go through the village, over the beck, and onto the drive of Colburn Hall. Turn left on a lane that becomes a streamside path. Go up the right-hand edge of a large field, under two power lines, and across the field beyond. Slant left down the third field to a signposted gate. A stony track leads to Hagg Farm.

Pass to left of a barn reconstruction, and along the top of the flood-plain banking, to enter the wood. Descend gradually to the riverbank, to cross two footbridges. A riverbank field leads to the sewage works. Pass left of these onto their track, and cross a cattle grid onto a railway footpath under trees.

This ends at the former station, past which is Station Bridge. Go down steps on the right, to pass under the bridge onto the Swaleside path. Pass above a wood, then down to the riverbank to Richmond Bridge. Cross the Swale, and turn right up cobbled Cornforth Hill. New Road leads to the Market Place.

RICHMOND: Leave by Finkle Street, and turn right at the end of Newbiggin to find a rising lane, Westfields. After 1¼ miles (2km) this becomes a track through Whitcliffe Wood, and then along the high side of the valley. Where this dips to East Applegarth, pass above the farm and join, for just 10m/yds, its tarred entrance track. A stile down left leads to the access track for Low Applegarth: this is crossed, to gap stiles across two wide fields to West Applegarth.

The valley-side track continues to a white cairn under Applegarth Scar. A mile (1.5 km) away, a road can be seen under the wooded side of Marske Moor: the way makes directly for this. A path slants down left, passing the top corner of a fenced enclosure to a hidden footbridge. Three stiles lead to a hedge-gap: the road is reached by a stile in the hedge. Turn left to MARSKE village.

Those equipped with the Yorkshire Dales North map can now reach Reeth by a tougher, but nicer route. Follow the Marske Beck upstream to a footbridge near Telfit Farm, and then to Helton. Climb the valley side to Prys House. Narrow moor paths lead to Owlands Farm, and to a track top above Cuckoo Hill. A footpath descends from White House to the Arkle Beck and Reeth.

Turn right at Marske's phone box, to a road marked 'unsuitable for motors'. At the end of the houses, head down to a stone footbridge (Pillmire Bridge). Cross, to the road beyond. A stile opposite leads to the foot of a long field. At the top, go round the right corner of an oak plantation to a gate onto the road. Turn left for 150m/yds to Hardstiles Top. A signpost points back right into the field. Cross the brow, to a signpost beyond. Turn left along the wall, and descend to pass to the right of Hollins Farm. The waymarked route slants down two fields to a footbridge beside Ellers cottage.

Turn right, around behind the cottage. Marked

stiles lead uphill, to the left of a field barn, to a track. Turn right for 30m/yds to a stile on the left. More stiles lead over the hill and down into the edge of Marrick.

A gate on the right is marked 'no access': go ahead, past stranded railway trucks, to more gap-stiles. At the track below turn right into MARRICK. A lane descends from the phone box to become a field edge path opening into the top of Steps Wood. The ancient flagstones lead down to Marrick Priory.

Go down the tarred access lane (or take an unway-marked field path above), to a stile onto the river-bank. The Swale-side footpath leads to Grinton Bridge, which is not crossed, and then to the road just outside Reeth. Cross Reeth Bridge, and then turn left to pass back underneath it onto beckside footpath. After 50m/yds a branch path leads up into the town.

Leave REETH by the Gunnerside road, to the top of its first climb. Just before the school, steps lead up into a walled path – no footpath sign. Above the school, slant up left through a wall gap to reach a corner of the walled path (Skelgate Lane). It's a green tunnel under various prickly plants, so that when a gate lets you out onto the grassland above, the Swaledale view is a sudden one.

For the next 2 miles (3km) the way will follow the tops of the walled fields, the bottom of the grassy moor. This is the best level from which to enjoy Swaledale, as well as offering fast and easy travel.

Follow the wall top up-valley for 20m/yds, then take a traversing path, past a cairn and above Riddings Farm to rejoin the wall. A clear track leads, after 800m/yds, down to Thirns Farm, where a new track continues up-valley, climbing gently then levelling. When it peters out, continue above walltops. A gap-stile looks down suddenly into Cringley Bottom.

This stream ravine has steep sides and no footbridge. A clear path slants down across the moor beyond, passing above Surrender Smelt Mill to road near Surrender Bridge. Go straight across onto a shooters' track.

Follow the track up the Old Gang Beck, forking left across Level House Bridge, to reach devastated stony ground at the moor top. A few steps short of the end of the stony spoil, cairns mark a much fainter track branching left. The track steepens, and takes a zigzag out to the left and back.

The track turns left again towards a sheep enclosure, but here we go straight downhill, on a stony spur that is the edge of a small re-entrant: Bunton Hush. Drop right, and go down inside it as it becomes a rocky ravine. Soon the left-hand wall becomes a small crag; a ruined building is just below. Here leave the ravine, traversing right on a small path.

After 100m/yds this starts to descend, through grass and scree, to meet a larger path. This leads up-valley, gently ascending, then becoming a narrow green track. Above the arched ruins of Blakethwaite Smelt Mill, a cairn marks a zigzag path that drops to the single-slab footbridge.

GUNNERSIDE GILL: Once over the stream, go down-valley on a green track for 100m/yds, then pick up a path that goes back right, then climbs left to the moor top to join a stony track. Cross the moor, and at a small culvert, take a muddy path on the left that bends right to rejoin the track at the top of the sharp valley of the East Gill (signpost).

Cross the track. The descending path is muddy at first, with one or two waymark poles. It becomes rocky and steep, to reach the mine buildings in the hollow of the valley. Traverse out right, crossing the Hind Hole Beck and where the path forks taking the higher one (Keld). This becomes a track, dropping past Crackpot Hall and traversing above the Swale Gorge before dropping again to a bridge over East Gill (waterfall below). The main route continues ahead, but a signed footpath drops left to a footbridge then rises to Keld.

East to West 3:

Westmorland

From Keld, return across the footbridge of the Swale, and turn left up the track into East Stonesdale farmyard. The lower gate ahead leads onto the farm's access track, which runs above the river to the moor road. A few steps up the road, take a footpath that runs along the top of Cotterby Scar overlooking the river. Above Low Bridge, it joins the rough track up to Smithy Holme. A rough path runs up slightly right, its line unclear until a high fingerpost appears ahead. It then runs along the bottom of a stone enclosure, and contours to reach the brink of the wooded gorge of the Whitsundale Beck. Once past the gorge, it drops to the stream. Waymarked gap-stiles lead to Ravenseat.

Cross the stone packhorse-bridge, and follow the stream bank to a ladder-stile. A small path leads up to a gated gap. Through this, follow the wall to the right, to the Ney Gill stream. 100m/yds upstream is the Ney Gill Signpost where the seasonal routes diverge. From here to Hartley Fell the route splits, with different permissive paths for different times of the year.

RED ROUTE (August-November): A path runs up to right of the stream, to reach a black shooters' hut. A bulldozed track continues over the moor. At its highest point turn off right onto a narrow peaty path with a single waymark pole. This leads gently uphill, north, past two cairns to the signpost south of Nine Standards Rigg.

BLUE ROUTE (May-July): Turn right, along the wall. The path turns left before the stream, and follows the valley side, above the stream, for 1½ miles (2.5km) with occasional waymark poles. At a fingerpost it turns uphill, to the right (north) of the incut Craygill Scar stream. As the slope eases it becomes a wide peaty trod, marked by widely-spaced poles, to the signpost in the col south of Nine Standards Rigg.

BLUE AND RED ROUTES COMBINED: Head 150m/yds on 340 degrees to a further signpost: this crossing is of deep peat hags, and if the mist is thick enough to require the compass, it'll be hard indeed to stay on this bearing – indeed, hard to stay on this ground, as it constantly tries to slide you sideways into a brown hole. The path leads past three cairns to the trig point, and then the viewpoint indicator, with the Nine Standards themselves just beyond.

The path descends west, then traverses 120m/yds south-west just to confuse people who look at their maps. It goes down over peat to a footbridge near a tall cairn, and then to the left of Faraday Gill in its little ravine. It slants left, to join a wall and the green track alongside. Here the Winter Route rejoins.

GREEN ROUTE (December-April): A path runs up to right of the stream, to reach a black shooters' hut. A bulldozed track continues over the moor. As the track descends, slant off right to join the road below. This is followed for 1½ miles (2.5km), to the regional boundary of Yorkshire and Cumbria at the top of the pass.

After another 300m/yds, a signpost (Rollinson Haggs) indicates a faint green track that runs north over grass and limestone lumps. Route-finding here is tricky in mist. After 800m/yds it starts to descend towards Dukerdale – a deep valley with limestone crags opposite. A stone wall is ahead. Turn half-right, north-east, and go down pathless grass to the wall, then follow it right, to a corner at the head of Dukerdale. The wall leads round the valley head and up to another corner. As it turns off left, contour forward on a small cairned path.

The path crosses the Rollinson Gill stream, then zigzags up beyond it to a ruin. Just above the ruin it meets a larger path at a Coast-to-Coast fingerpost.

Turn down the new path, and follow it as it becomes a green track and rejoins the wall below.

ALL ROUTES NOW REJOINED AT HARTLEY FELL: The track leads on down the wall, becoming stony, then slanting right to a gate and the road top. This road can be followed to Hartley village, where a left turn finds a tarred path across fields to Kirkby Stephen.

However, a more interesting, more difficult way turns left onto the farm track signposted 'Ladthwaite'. After the cattle grid contour forward, above spoil heaps, before descending a grassy slope to rejoin the track. At Ladthwaite, take a stile on the right and head down alongside Ladthwaite Beck. This passes around the base of Birkett Hill, then bends right to start dropping into its gorge: here contour out left and go down above the streamside trees to a gate.

Descend, and contour through the wood on cow trods with a view to the limestone crag opposite. When a wall blocks the way, go up to a gate beside a field barn. The wall on the right leads along a green lane, across the disused railway, and down to a track. Turn right, through a wood, to a footbridge, and follow the riverbank of Eden downstream. A fine packhorse bridge leads into the town.

Leave KIRKBY STEPHEN southwards, turning off the A685 onto a parallel lane on the right. This leads through Greenriggs Farm and between the piers of a disused railway bridge. Turn right through a gate into a field, and uphill to a waymarked stile (yellow-top pole). The field path, not distinct, goes up a small dry valley to two more stiles and the bridge under the railway.

Head slightly right past a field barn, and then bend right to cross diagonally to the back left corner of the field. Take the road left to a junction, then back right to a ladder stile. Go up the field with a wall on the right, and still with no clear path. At the top of the slope the wall bends away to the right: here bend left around the curve of the slope, and descend south-west to a signpost near a wall corner. Go down, with the wall on the right, to SMARDALE BRIDGE.

Immediately after the bridge, a permissive path arrow points up right. Go up to the abandoned railway, and follow it to the right, for 200m/yds, before crossing on the bridge. Continue along the railway to an empty house, then follow the wall up Begin Hill. Cross at a waymarked stile after 3/4 mile (1 km), and continue to follow the wall, now on its right. After a gate a clear track starts, and leads (still with wall on left) past Bents Farm to a gate on the left beside a barn.

In the field beyond, the faint track follows the left-hand wall past the small swamp of Ewefell Mire, then moves across to the opposite side to reach the moor road. Turn right along the road for 1 1/2 miles (2km), past Mazon Wath, to a junction on high grassland below limestone scars.

Turn left, down the Raisbeck road, for 500m/yds, then bear right on a faint track above Spear Pots pond. After 200m/yds a small path with occasional waymark poles leads left, to a gap-stile. A green path, through heather with scattered thorns, leads to a stony track, then to the road at Stony Head. Bear left to pass the farm, and bend left again passing Sunbiggin Farm. After 600m/yds downhill, the road reaches Acres Farm.

A sign on the right indicates the bridleway. This crosses fields, always on the same level and always westwards, through no fewer than ten gap-stiles to Keld Lane. Cross this rough track right, to a bridleway sign. Cross a field, with a fence on the right, to Scar Side Farm.

Just past the farm, a footpath sign indicates a muddy track on the right. Follow it through three fields, then continue in the same direction, through a wall gap and along a green way between walls, then passing to right of a thicket. Walls on the left guide to the stile onto Street Lane. Turn left for 150m/yds, for a long field leading into ORTON.

Cross the first street onto a further footpath for the hotel and shop.

The street opposite the Post Office leads to the stocks. Turn up left to the church. A signpost (Shap) points to left of the building, between the grave-stones, to a stile into a muddy field. Turn half-right to a wall corner, and follow this wall's direction, which is north. Stiles marked with white paint lead to the left of Bullflat and up fields beyond. Take the left-hand of two empty gateways, to pass a lone tree beside the wall. At this field top, don't take the empty gateway ahead, but the marked stile 20m/yds left. A stile is in the top left corner of the field above.

A faint path leads straight out onto the heather moor, and into a grassy groove that becomes a dry valley. Go down this, to pass the small but ancient cairn that is Robin Hood's Grave. After another 100m/yds, a wall blocks the valley. Turn left, along-side it, to cross another sharp little valley.

At the top of the following rise the wall turns right, north. Now slant away from it, to cross Lyvennet Beck 100m/yds out from the wall. Waymarks lead up the opposite slope past a large erratic boulder to the top of WICKER STREET. Here is an ancient monument sign, with, just to north, an area of lime-stone pavement with two trees.

Go down slightly north of west, to pass the end of a pine plantation, and go up for 100m/yds to a faint green track leading across to the right (sign and waymark where you join the track). It passes to the right of a walled enclosure with a few trees, and joins a much clearer track coming out of the enclosure. This leads to ODDENDALE.

Turn left onto a wide gravel road. Where this bends left, use wide wooden steps ahead to cross the sunken track leading into the huge Hardendale Quarry. The wall beyond leads to a stile, then bends left, downhill. Leave it to cross a field of scattered boulders, passing along the foot of a low limestone outcrop to the road at The Nab.

Cross at footpath signs to a gate. Cross the brow of the hill to the motorway, and follow this right, to cross a footbridge. Turn right, and cross fields north-west from stile to stile to a walled track. This leads down into Shap.

East to West 4:

Lakeland

SHAP: Leave the main street at the ancient library, and turn right in the back lane to find a footpath running west. It passes the upstanding Goggleby Stone to reach a walled track. Turn right for 50m/yds, then left in Keld Lane to another walled track on the right. This ends at a road junction, with Shap Abbey down left.

Cross the bridge on the right, which is Abbey Bridge (with the Abbey itself up left) and turn right to a ladder stile just above. Cross the field, slanting up to join the wall above for another ladder stile. Follow the wall on the left till it turns away left, then cross the field corner ahead to a third ladder stile and a lower stile beyond. Turn down the tarred lane to its corner, where two more stiles lead between farm buildings. What sort of stiles? Ladder ones. This half-mile has half the ladders of the entire trip.

Straight down the field is Parish Crag Bridge, hidden in trees. Turn slightly right along a fence, which becomes a wall leading below Goodcroft to its access track and a road corner near Rosgill Bridge.

Immediately cross a ladder stile on the left and go up a boggy field to a road. Turn right, to a footpath sign at the driveway of Rawhead. The way passes left of this house, and traverses from stile to stile, just south of west, aiming into the huge hole of Mardale. After passing below the restored barn of

Highpark Buildings, don't cross the stile ahead but turn down the fence to the riverside.

Head upstream, past Park Bridge and Thornthwaite Force (waterfall) to Naddle Bridge. Cross both bridge and road, to a footpath into woods. A left fork after 60m/yds leads into BURNBANKS.

Take the tarred track slanting up right, turning sharply right on an upper track that turns back left to leave the forest. This track, and then its continuation path, lead for 4 miles (6km) along the north shore of Haweswater Reservoir. After passing below a plantation opposite the promontory of Speaking Crag, cross the stone footbridge of Randale Beck.

Now a grass path heads up towards the rocky end of Kidsty Howes. It passes to the left of the lowest rocks, then slants up right, to take a line up the spur just right of its crest. A gentle path leads up the ridge to Kidsty Pike.

In mist, the next half-mile (1 km) is confusing. The path from Kidsty's small cairn curves round left, with steep drops to its left, and joins a broad path with a wall beside it. Turn sharply back right, with the wall on the left. Where the wall turns up left, continue downhill on a broad stony path, watching out for a side-path on the right. If you find yourself about to descend steep zigzags, you have passed the side-path: go back to the previous cairn.

The path descends gently north-west, and joins a wall below just as it becomes a fence. Path and fence lead to Satura Crag. Here the fence becomes a wall again, and it's better to stay in touch with this wall rather than following the path as it wanders aimlessly to the right and then back.

After a gate, the path goes down just left of the grassy ridge line to pass above Angle Tarn, and traverse the top of a steep slope above the Kirkstone road. After going down a little stream valley, go straight across a five-way path junction (Boredale Hause). The path, uncomfortably steep and eroded in descent, slants down to the settlement of Rooking. A lane crosses the valley floor to PATTERDALE.

Leave Patterdale by a track past the toilets. It bends right, to a footpath on the left. This goes through a wood and climbs with a wall on the right to a kissing gate. It continues slightly uphill to cross Hag Beck at stepping-stones. At the foot of the ridge of St Sunday Crag, a stile on the right leads down to a road.

Turn left, and where the road bends right, go ahead through a gate on the track up the south side of Grisedale. It diminishes to path for a long and steepening climb. At the valley head it forks. The left branch leads in 50m/yds to the outflow of Grisedale Tarn.

Cross the stream, and go round to left of the tarn on a path that slants up to Grisedale Hause. Go through the pass, and down a pitched path to cross the floor of the upper combe of Hause Moss. As the path steepens again, a side-path out to the right is a more interesting descent route. It traverses through broken ground. When open grassy (or brackeny) slopes are below, go down to the stream below. The path reforms on its right bank. It rejoins the main path at the stream junction 800 feet below (250m vertical).

A stony track leads down to the A591 near the Travellers' Rest. Go across into the lane, and across the river turn left, to pass the track-end of Thorny How Youth Hostel. Turn left at Easedale Road into GRASMERE.

Leave the village by the Easedale Road, following it to its end after the Lancrigg Guest House. The rough track on the right is signed 'Far Easedale'. After 50m/yds is a track junction where you could turn right for the higher crossing over Helm Crag. The track ahead is stony between high walls and under branches, and leads into the sequestered little valley of Far Easedale. The path recrosses the stream on its final climb to the valley head. The pass is marked by a small cairn, and the iron posts of an empty gateway.

The path ahead descends briefly, to a fork after 50m/yds. The left branch is the more dependable in mist. It keeps to the left of most of the bog, and crosses below the broken ground of Birks Crag before slanting up to meet Flour Gill (stream). After this it's a straight pull up to the second pass, Greenup Edge.

The descent path is not altogether clear, the cairns that mark it are widely-spaced, and there are crag-tops to the left. A compass-bearing will help: 345

degrees. A grassy platform on the left is the summit of Lining Crag. The path descends to the right of the crag, steeply, and runs down Greenup Valley to join Langstrathdale below. Stay to the right of the river as the path becomes a walled track. Ignore the first stone bridge on the left, which leads to Stonethwaite; ¾ mile (1km) later, a second leads into ROSTHWAITE.

Take the second tarred lane on the right, opposite the Royal Oak Hotel. When the lane turns left behind Yew Tree Farm, take an unsigned track on the right for 20m/yds, and turn left onto a field foot-path along the back of the village. After the first stile, cross a field corner to the right, to a way-marked gate. Pass to left of the cottage ahead, onto a road with Peat Howe Bridge just to the right.

Cross the bridge, and pass along the front of the youth hostel onto the riverside path. This leads through a wood, then open fields, and drops into the back of a car park at SEATOLLER.

Turn right, up the road to the end of the village, then right again through a gate onto the old road up Honister Pass. This heads out above the path you came in on to give views down Borrowdale. Then it turns back left and up into the pass. After a mile (1.5km) it runs into the tarred road, but leaves it again on the right after 100m/yds. It rejoins the road to reach the pass just below the youth hostel.

HONISTER HAUSE: Stay on the motor road to pass the Slate Company buildings, then turn back left through a gate. At a masonry cairn the tramway strikes uphill: the new path takes a line further right, before rejoining the tramway higher up. This ascends arrow-straight, rising onto an embankment on the level ground above.

MISTY WEATHER WAY (avoiding Hay Stacks)

Turn left off the embankment onto a wide, cairned path. This climbs gently south, then bends south-west as it slants up below a line of low outcrops. As it turns south again, look out for a much smaller cairned path branching off on the right – this is easily missed.

The new path, marked with small cairns, traverses (neither gaining nor losing height) on bearing 230 degrees. Having rounded the shallow valley head, it crosses the remains of a fence and descends into the deep-cut stream slot of Loft Beck. The ravine is steep and uncomfortable.

At the bottom of the ravine, Loft Beck leads down to the main Ennerdale stream. Follow this down to a footbridge. Don't cross (unless you want to visit Wasdale), but take the path to the right, past Black Sail Youth Hostel. Where the path bends up right towards Black Sail Pass, a gate ahead leads into the forest and onto a forest road. After a mile (1.5km), this runs above a footbridge on the left, which is ignored. After a second mile, a side-track on the left leads down to a track bridge over Liza Beck.

For the BETTER ROUTE BY HAY STACKS, the tramway continues downhill to a slate building among the stonepiles of the old Dubs Quarry. Go downhill to meet the stream at a path crossing. The path leads immediately right of the crag knoll Little Round How, and through rocky ground to the outflow of Blackbeck Tarn. It continues across the top of the steep slope overlooking Buttermere to pass to right of Innominate Tarn to the summit of HAY STACKS.

A recently built path gives a clear line down westwards to the pass of Scarth Gap, avoiding the various small and scrambly crags. Turn left for 150m/yds, and as the ground steepens, look for a small path traversing out of the pass on the right. This slants down across scree and through the corner of a forest, to join the forest road. Continue east for a mile (1.5km), when a side-track back left leads down to a track bridge over Liza Beck.

A waymarked path leads down the further riverbank. After ³/₄ mile (1.3km) it moves away from the river to join a green track. After 150m/yds, opposite the pool of Moss Dub, it leaves the track on the right – not waymarked. After another 800m/yds, it joins a forest road to cross Woundell Beck.

After 200m/yds, take a track on the right through a triple-gate out of the trees, and at once turn left over a ladder stile marked 'Lakeside Path'. This leads very pleasantly along the south shore of Ennerdale Water, with a slight scramble under Anglers' Crag. Do not go through the gate at the foot of the lake, but head up along the wall to the left to pass above Crag Farm. Move onto a forest track just above, and take a green track on the right in front of more trees. This crosses the Ehen on a long footbridge, and runs out along a driveway to the road. Turn left for ENNERDALE BRIDGE.

Leave over the bridge, and take the hill road (Calder Bridge) for a stiff climb to a cattle grid and open grassland. After a stone circle on the left (a fake) a footpath sign points down right. A made path runs along the bottom of the enchanting little valley of Nannycatch.

Keep left, beside the stream, and where the valley divides after ¾ mile (1 km), take the left branch, passing under the distinctive Raven Crag. On reaching forest, take the forest road up right for 300m/yds, and then bear right onto an old, neglected track climbing steeply. It zigzags, crossing a high forest road to a five-way junction where two galvanised tanks lurk under the branches. Turn sharp left, uphill and north-west, to a stile and open hill. A faint path leads to the eastern, and then along the ridge to the western summit of Dent Fell. The North Sea fills the view ahead.

Go down beside a broken wall into the forest below. Where the downward tree-gap ends, a sign (Black How) points left for 60m/yds to a descending forest road.

Cross the road below, and turn left behind Black How Farm. A rough road leads to the river bridge into CLEATOR. Turn left in the main street for 20m/yds, and take the street opposite. This bends right past the cricket pitch, where a gravel path leads ahead. Turn right onto the tarred trackbed of a former railway.

Where tarred paths meet beside Moor Row turn left, and go under three road bridges. Now the railway passes over a farm track, and here turn off on the right at a decorative metal waymark, to pass below the railway. Follow the track, which becomes faint, across a field to a grey gate. Now go round to the right of a small swamp or pool to a waymarked field gate. Turn right along the fence beyond, and follow it to a stile near Stanley Pond – the pond isn't visible, just lots of reeds.

Turn left after the stile, to a bridge under the railway. Go up to a track, and follow this up past Bell House to the B5345. Cross onto another track, that curves right to pass between the buildings of Demesne.

Now take the track to the left, which becomes a green way between hedges. Cross the road at Lanehead, for the lane into SANDWITH.

Turn right, onto a private road of the Trinity House lighthouse authority. After 600m/yds, fork right onto a track which leads to the cliffs. Turn left along the clifftop: the path runs on one side or the other of the cliff edge fence, and is waymarked as 'Cumbria Coastal Path'. So the walking is without navigational interest, but is enjoyable in every other respect, for the last three miles to ST BEES.

Contacts

TOURIST INFORMATION

WHITEHAVEN 01946 695678; EGREMONT 01946 820693; SEATOLLER 01768 777294 (seasonal); GRASMERE 01539 435245; ULLSWATER 01768 482414; KIRKBY STEPHEN 01768 371199; RICH-MOND 01748 825994/850252; NORTHALLERTON 01609 776864 (seasonal); DANBY 01287 660654 (seasonal); WHITBY 01947 602674.

ACCOMMODATION LISTINGS

Stilwell's National Trail Companion – covers all National Trails and others including the Coast-to-Coast, from bookshops or else phone 0171 739 7179; Coast-to-Coast Accommodation Guide: £3, from North York Moors Adventure Centre, Park House, Ingleby Cross, Northallerton DL6 3PE 01609 882571; Coast-to-Coast B&B Guide: £2.50, from Mrs Doreen Whitehead, Butt House, Keld, Richmond DL11 6LJ 01748 886374.

HAULAGE CONTRACTORS

These will carry your luggage (and, if necessary, you) between overnight stopping-points along the walk. They also offer secure car parking with minibus service to and from St Bees and Robin Hood's Bay.

Bee-jay International Walking Tours: 4 Peareth Grove, Sunderland SR6 9NL 0191 548 7060.

Coast-to-Coast Packhorse: West View Farmhouse, Hartley, Kirkby Stephen CA17 4JH 017683 71680.

White Knight (In Step): 35 Cokeham Road, Lancing BN15 0AE 01903 766475.

BOOKING BUREAUS

Pre-booked overnight accommodation for the entire crossing:

Bee-jay Tours (see above); Coast-to-Coast Pack-horse (see above); Jolly Farmers: 63 High Street, Kirkby Stephen CA17 4SH 017683 71063; YHA Coast-to-Coast Booking Bureau (in B&Bs and Youth Hostels) 01629 825850.

TRAVEL INFORMATION: Rail: 0345 484950; Bus: 0891 910910; Cumbria Travelline 01228 606000; Stagecoach Cumbria 01946 63222; United (York-shire) 01325 468771; Tees Bus Infoline 01947 602146; National Express 0990 808080.

Bus timetables (free):

Lakeland Explorer: PO Box 17, Tangier St, White-haven CA28 7XF; Dales Connections: Yorkshire Dales National Park, Colvend, Hebden Road, Grassington, Skipton BD23 5LB; Moors Connec-tions: North York Moors National Park, the Old Vicarage, Bondgate, Helmsley, York YO6 5BP.

WEATHER

Lake District (one-day) 01768 775757; North-west

England 0891 500 419; North-east England 0891 500 418.

What Next?

Once the blisters heal up, you may start thinking about another long walk. If you want something a bit easier, I would suggest the West Highland Way (100 miles/160km). It's well waymarked and mostly on broad tracks near civilisation, but through spectacular mountain scenery. For something similarly rough, but short enough for a single week, look at the Cumbria Way (100 miles/160km, unwaymarked) or the Two Moors Way (100 miles/160km, waymarked).

In an assessment by *Strider*, the journal of the Long Distance Walkers' Association, the title 'best long-distance walk' was shared by the Coast-to-Coast and the 170-mile/270km Offa's Dyke Way along the Welsh border.

For a tougher mountain route, with low-level alternatives, I commend the Welsh Coast-to-Coast (Snowdonia to Gower). Its 220 unwaymarked miles (350km) are described in John Gillham's guidebook. While if the Coast-to-Coast was altogether too soft, try the Scottish Coast-to-Coast: no waymarks, no guidebook, and the problems of devising and following a route are added to the midges, mountains, and bogs of the wild Highlands.

Acknowledgements

Busy people all the way across England shared their time and knowledge. Thanks to Bill Wheeler (FE Grizedale); LDNP rangers, particularly Scott Henderson & Ian Clemmett; Dick Capel and Phil Gray (ECCP); Simon Webb (English Nature: alas, still no limestone pavement); YDNPA information officers; Peter Penny (N Yorks CC); and Karl Gerhardsen (NYMNP); to Robert Whittington for the route through Lancrigg Wood; to the Ordnance Survey and Stirling Surveys for maps; and to Alfred Wainwright, for starting it all off.

Other Dalesman titles for walkers
Walking and Trail Guides
LAKE DISTRICT, EASTERN FELLS Paddy Dillon £5.99
LAKE DISTRICT, WESTERN FELLS Paddy Dillon £5.99
WHITE PEAK Martin Smith £4.99
DARK PEAK John Gillham £4.99
NORTH PENNINES Alan Hall £4.99
SOUTH PENNINES John Gillham £4.99
CLEVELAND WAY Martin Collins £4.99
PENNINE WAY Terry Marsh £4.99

Walks Around Series: Peak District
BAKEWELL Martin Smith £1.99
BUXTON Andrew McCloy £1.99
CASTLETON John Gillham £1.99
MATLOCK Martin Smith £1.99

Walks Around Series: Lake District
AMBLESIDE Tom Bowker £1.99
HAWKSHEAD Mary Welsh £1.99
KESWICK Dawn Gibson £1.99
WINDERMERE Robert Gambles £1.99
Pub and Tea Shop Walks Series
LAKE DISTRICT Terry Marsh £5.99
NORTH YORK MOORS & COAST Richard Musgrave £5.99
PEAK DISTRICT John Morrison £5.99
YORKSHIRE DALES Richard Musgrave £5.95
Safety for Walkers
MOUNTAIN SAFETY Kevin Walker £4.99
MAP READING Robert Matkin £3.50

CUMBRIA AND LAKE DISTRICT MAGAZINE features walking
in each monthly issue £1.00

Available from all good bookshops. In case of difficulty contact
Dalesman Publishing Company, Clapham Via Lancaster
LA2 8EB. Tel: 015242 51225